Making felt toys and glove puppets

Making felt toys and glove puppets

Suzy Ives

B T Batsford Limited   London
Charles T Branford Company   Massachusetts

To John

© Suzy Ives 1971
First published 1971
7134 2652 7
Branford SBN 8231 5029 1

Designed by Charlotte Baron
Filmset in Univers Medium by Keyspools Limited Golborne Lancs
Printed in Great Britain by Taylor Garnett Evans Watford Herts
Bound by William Brendon and Son Limited Tiptree Essex
for the publishers
B T Batsford Limited 4 Fitzhardinge Street London W1
and Charles T Branford Company 18 Union Street Newton Centre
Massachusetts 02159

Contents

Introduction		6
Hand puppets	The basic shape	8
Glove puppet	Girl	9
Glove puppet	Boy	14
Glove puppet	Lion	18
Glove puppet	Tiger	22
Glove puppet	Penguin	26
Glove puppet	Skeleton	30
Finger puppet	Bear	34
Finger puppet	Clown	36
Finger puppet	Indian girl	38
Finger puppets	Ideas	40
Stuffed animal	Mouse	42
Stuffed animal	Hedgehog	46
Stuffed animal	Oozle	50
Stuffed animal	Snake	54
Stuffed animal	Tortoise	58
Stuffed animal	Owl	62
Stuffed animal	Broccoli bird	66
Stuffed animal	Lizard	74
Stuffed animal	Dragon	78
More ideas		86
Suppliers		88

Introduction

All the puppets and animals in this book are best made in felt, although other materials could be used.

A 305 mm (12 in.) square of felt is more than enough for the basic shape of each glove puppet, and for small hands a 230 mm (9 in.) square would do.

The mice, hedgehogs, owls and tortoises need less felt for for the basic shapes, (at least three mice can be made out of a 305 mm (12 in.) square). The lizard and the snake however, need two 230 mm (9 in.) squares each. The bird needs two 305 mm (12 in.) squares and the dragon needs two strips of felt, each 705 × 305 mm (16 × 12 in.).

After making two or three toys there will be quite a useful collection of scraps of felt left over. These can be used for the decoration of other toys, but to begin with I suggest that you have at least these colours among the basic starting materials: One square each of pale pink, white, black and red: two squares of bright pink, and of course, the colours chosen for the basic shapes.

Any buttons, sequins or beads collected are very useful for decoration, and lengths of wool and string can be used for the hair, manes and tails. I have used rug wool for this, which is thicker than ordinary knitting wool, and is very easy to stick and sew, but there is no reason for not using any scraps of wool that you can find.

To stick the faces and decorations onto the toys a *rubber solution glue* must be used. *Copydex* is a good one. Many other glues tend to become hard and will not bend as you use the puppets. PVA adhesives are not very satisfactory.

Kapok is very good for stuffing the animals, but for the lizard and snake it is very effective to use UNcooked rice; this makes them heavy and more realistic. (It also means that you have nourishment on hand should you fall on hard times!)

The following things should be ready before starting to make the felt toys:
The felt
A *sharp* pair of scissors
A needle
Cotton
Stuffing (if you are making an animal)
A knitting needle or pencil to push the stuffing in
Copydex glue
Rug wool
This book

Hand Puppets   The basic shape

The glove for all the hand puppets is basically the same. Pin two squares of felt together and put your hand onto them. Draw round your hand leaving plenty of room for the fingers. Cut the glove out and sew the two halves together using blanket stitch. *Do not forget to leave the opening to put your hand in.*

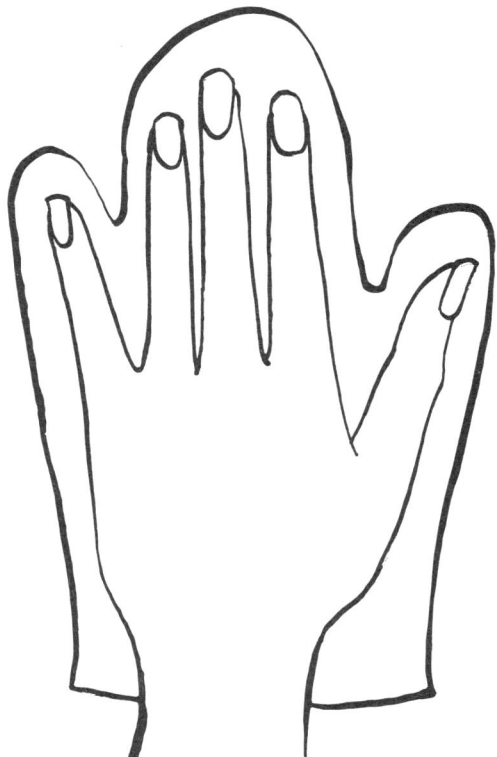

Figure 1

Follow the instructions for each toy carefully. It is important to assemble the puppets and animals in the order shown.

Glove Puppet   Girl

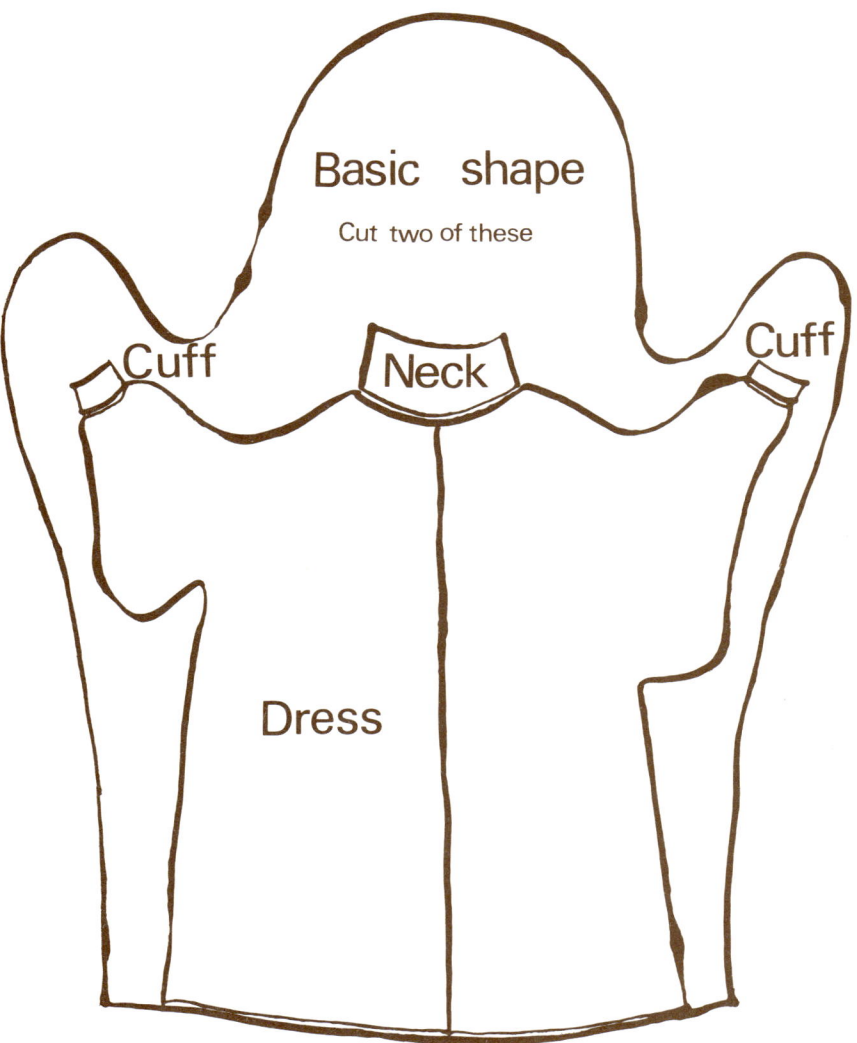

Figure 2

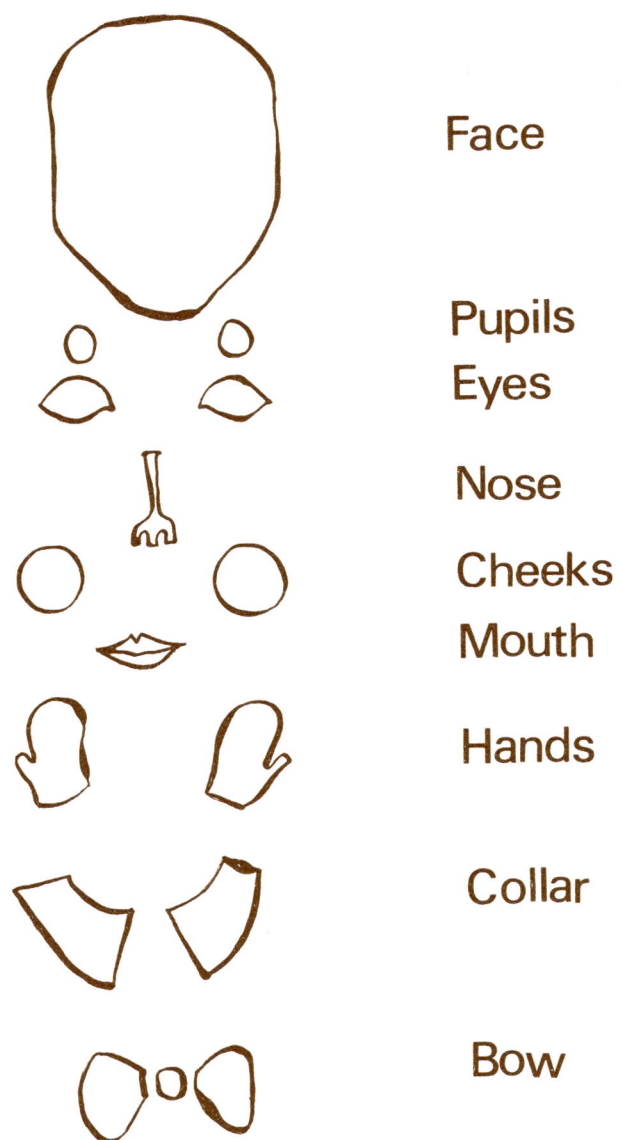

Face

Pupils
Eyes

Nose

Cheeks

Mouth

Hands

Collar

Bow

Figure 3

Cut out and sew the basic glove shape
Cut out all the features and decorations as shown in *figure 3*, and the dress in *figure 2*
1 Stick the pupils onto the eyes
2 Stick the eyes onto the face
3 Stick the nose onto the face

4 Stick the mouth onto the face
5 Stick the cheeks onto the face
6 Draw in the eyebrows,
with a black ballpoint pen

7   Stick the face onto the glove
8   Stick the neck onto the glove
9   Stick the dress onto the glove
10 Stick the cuffs onto the glove
11 Stick the hands onto the glove
12 Stick the collar and bow onto the dress

Figure 4

11

13 Cut six strands of rug wool, each about 405 mm (16 in.) long

14 Sew through the middle of each strand to the middle of the forehead

Remember to sew through only one thickness of the glove

15 Gather the strands together at each side of the face and overstitch them to the glove

16 Plait the two bunches of wool and tie the ends with matching thread

17 Fluff out the ends of the plaits

Figure 5

Figure 6

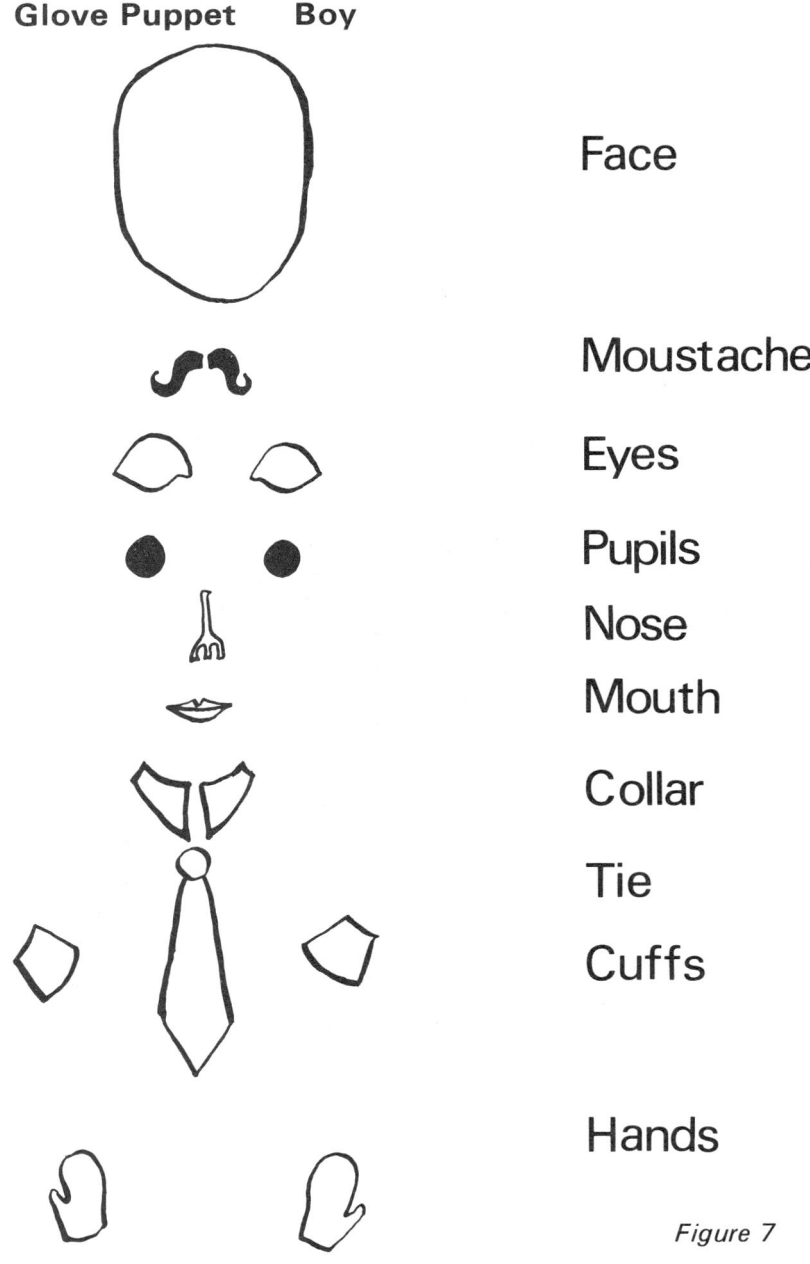

Figure 7

Cut out and sew the basic glove shape
Cut out all the features and decorations in *figure 7*
1   Stick the pupils to the eyes

2   Stick the eyes to the face
3   Stick the nose to the face
4   Stick the mouth to the face
5   Stick the face to the glove
6   Draw in the eyebrows,
with a black ballpoint pen

7   Stick the collar to the glove
8   Stick the tie to the glove
9   Stick the cuffs to the glove
10 Stick the hands to the glove

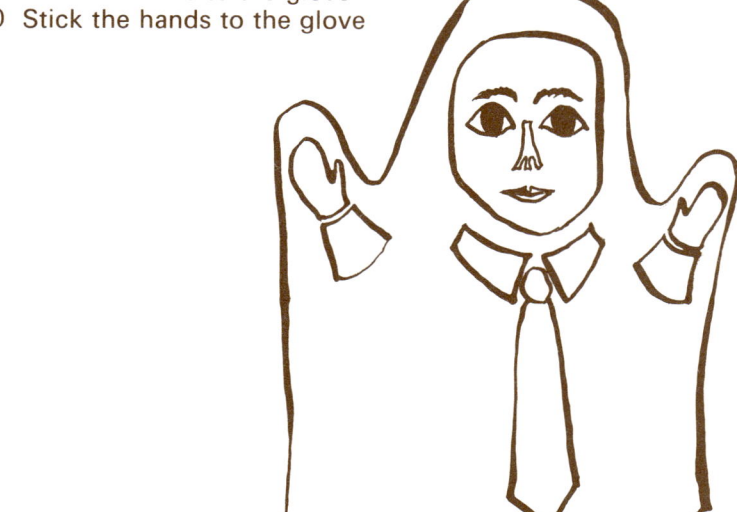

Figure 8

11 Cut six strands of rug wool, each about 125 mm (5 in.) long
12 Sew them to the middle of the top of the forehead
13 Arrange the strands as in *figure 9a*
14 Trim the strands to the correct length
15 Stick the strands down with a little glue

Figure 9a

Glove Puppet   Man

Figure 9b

Follow the instructions for the boy up to number 10
11 Stick the moustache on
12 Cut six strands of rug wool, each about 125 mm (5 in.) long
13 Sew them to the top of the forehead a little to the right
14 Arrange them as in *figure 9b*
15 Trim the strands and stick them down with a little glue

Figure 10

Glove Puppet   Lion

Cut out and sew the basic glove shape
Cut out all the features and paws in *figure 11*

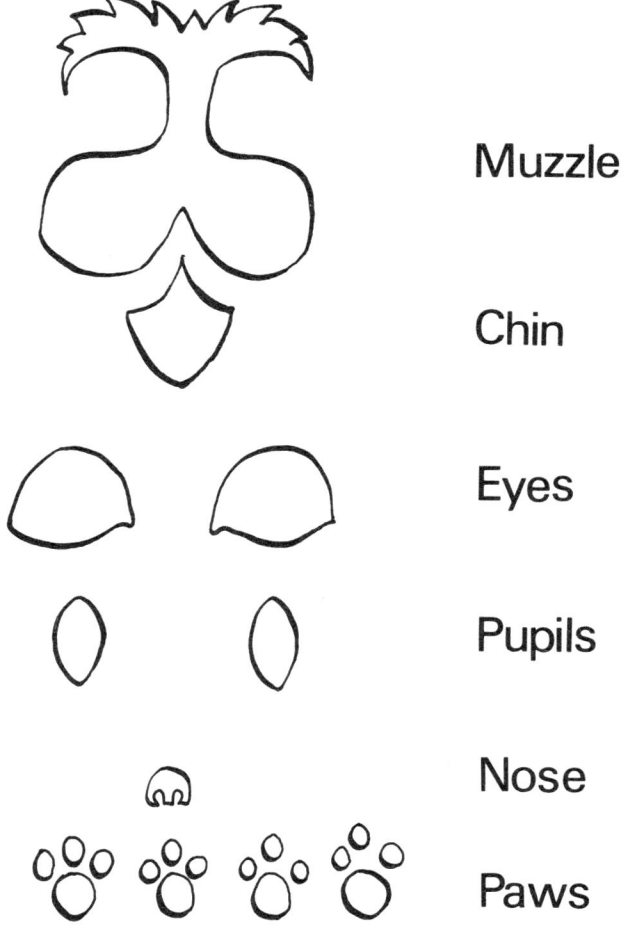

Figure 11

1 Stick the pupil to the eye
2 Stick the nose to the muzzle

3 Stick the muzzle to the glove
4 Stick the eyes to the glove
5 Stick the chin to the glove
6 With a black ballpoint pen, draw three small circles each side of the nose. From each of these three circles, draw a whisker. Draw small vertical lines on the chin
7 Stick the paws to the glove

Figure 12

8   Take a very long strand of rug wool, loop it and catch stitch it to the glove as shown in *figure 13*

Remember to sew through only one thickness of the glove

9   Continue looping and stitching until the wool surrounds the lion's face. Fasten off securely
10   Cut three strands of rug wool, each about 200 mm (8 in.) long
11   Tie them together and plait them
12   Tie the end of the plait with matching thread
13   Sew the plaited wool to the back of the glove
14   Fluff out the end of the plait

Figure 13

Figure 14

Glove Puppet   Tiger

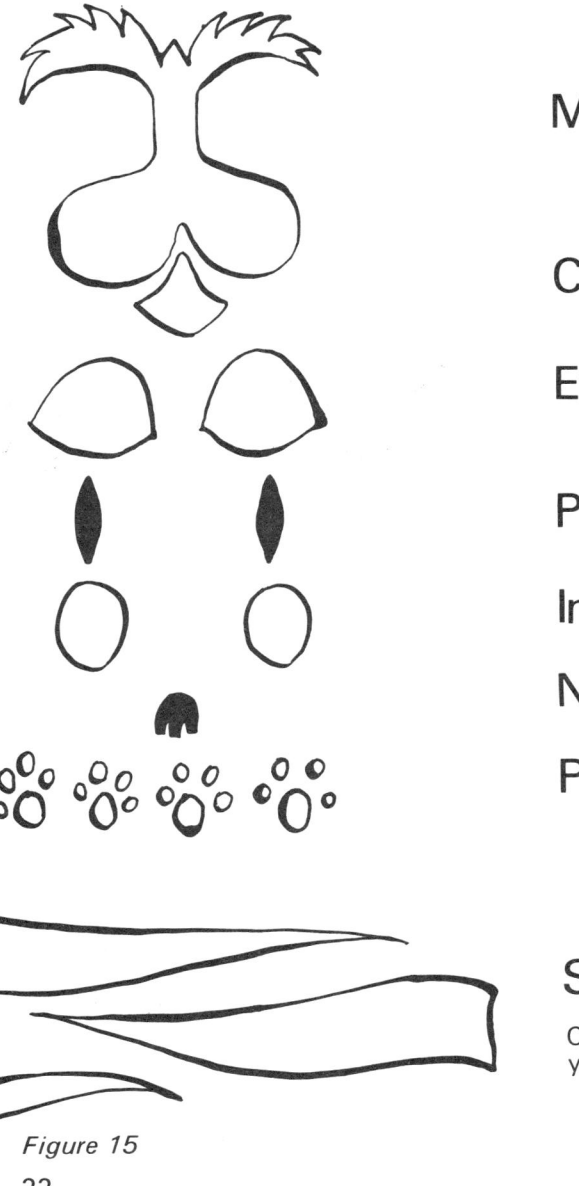

Muzzle

Chin

Eyes

Pupils

Inner eyes

Nose

Paws

Stripes

Cut these as you need them

Figure 15

Cut out and sew the basic glove shape
Cut out all the features and paws in *figure 15. Do not cut the stripes yet*
1 Stick the pupil to the inner eye
2 Stick the inner eye to the outer eye
3 Stick the nose to the muzzle

4 Stick the muzzle to the glove
5 Stick the eyes to the glove
6 Stick the chin to the glove
7 With a black ballpoint pen, draw five little circles each side of the nose. Draw small vertical lines on the chin
8 Stick the paws to the glove

Figure 16

9 Cut out the stripes, making them as thick or as thin as you like
10 Stick the stripes to the glove
11 Trim the edges of the stripes
12 Make a plait of two yellow strands of wool and one black
13 Sew the plait to the back of the glove
14 Fluff out the end of the plait

Figure 17

Figure 18

If you want to make a leopard, simply stick spots instead of stripes onto the glove

Glove Puppet   Penguin

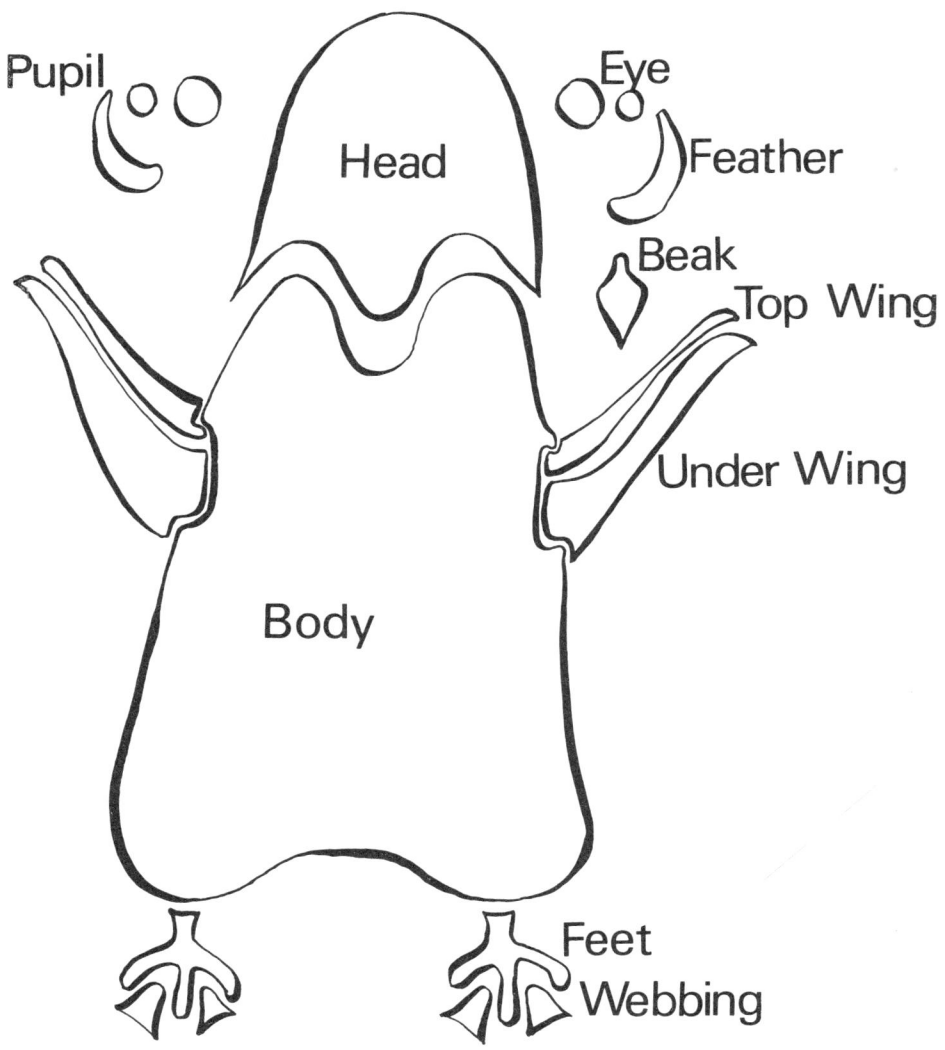

Figure 19

Cut out and sew the basic glove shape
Cut out all the pieces in *figure 19*
1   Stick the body to the glove
2   Stick the top wings to the glove

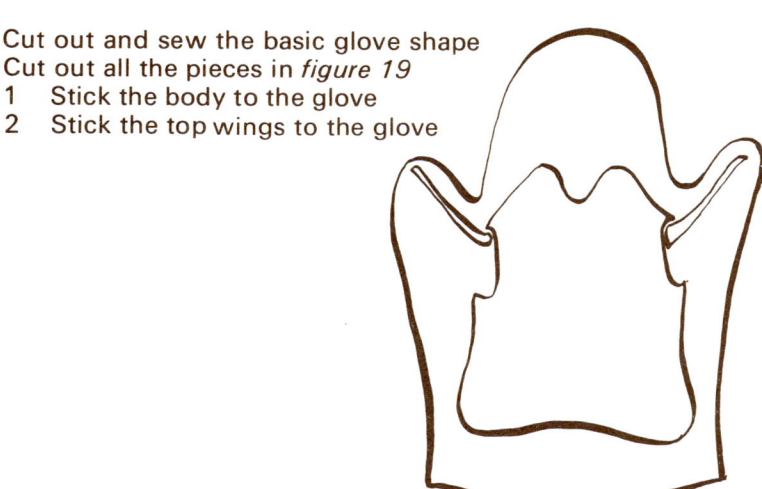

3   Stick the under wings to the glove

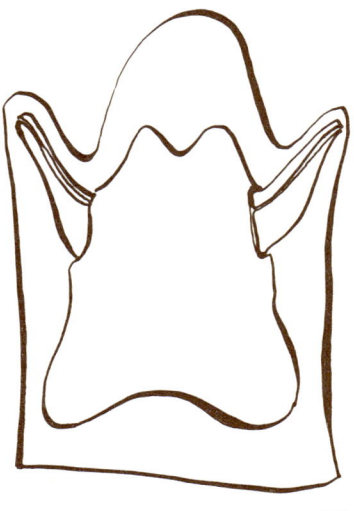

Figure 20

4 Stick the pupils to the eyes
5 Stick the eyes to the head
6 Stick the feathers to the head
7 Stick the beak to the head
8 Stick the head to the glove
9 Draw two small dots on the beak, with a black ballpoint pen

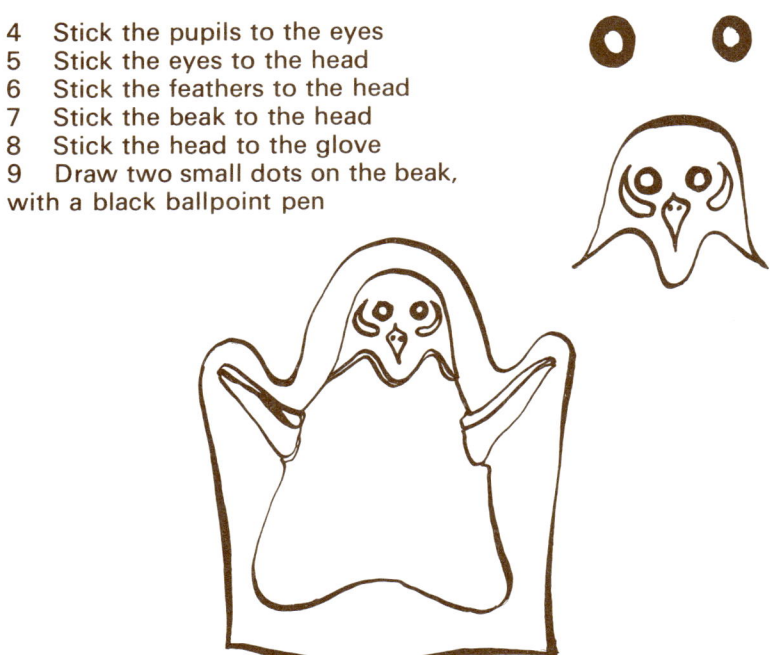

10 Stick the feet to the glove
11 Stick the webbing between the toes

Figure 21

Figure 22

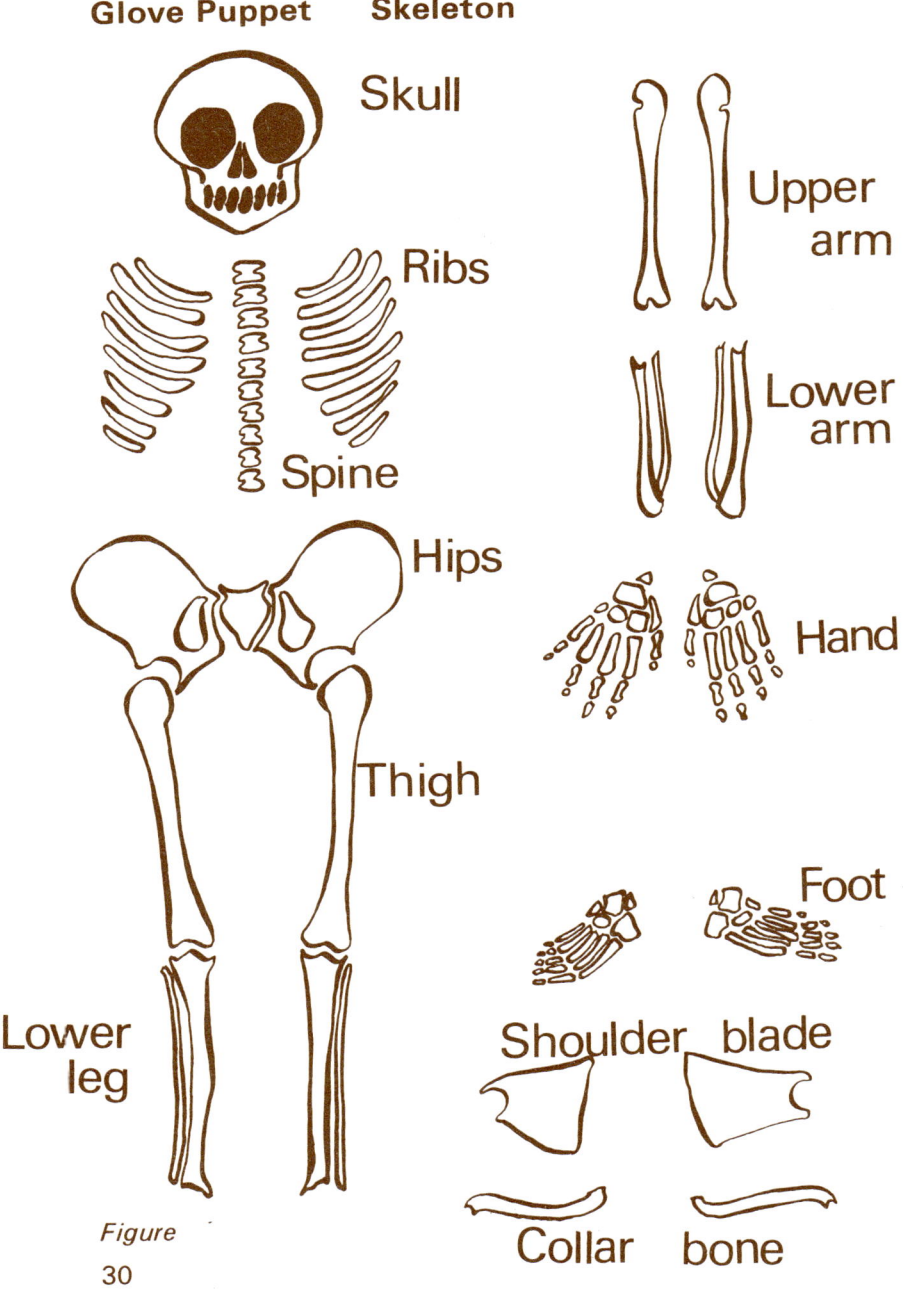

Figure 30

Cut out the basic glove shape, making the glove long enough to come well over your wrist
Sew the glove
Cut out all the pieces in *figure 23*
1   Stick the eyes, nose and teeth to the skull

2   Stick the skull to the glove
3   Stick the spine to the glove
4   Stick the shoulder-blades to the glove
5   Stick the hips to the glove
6   Stick the thighs and lower legs to the glove
7   Stick the upper and lower arms to the glove

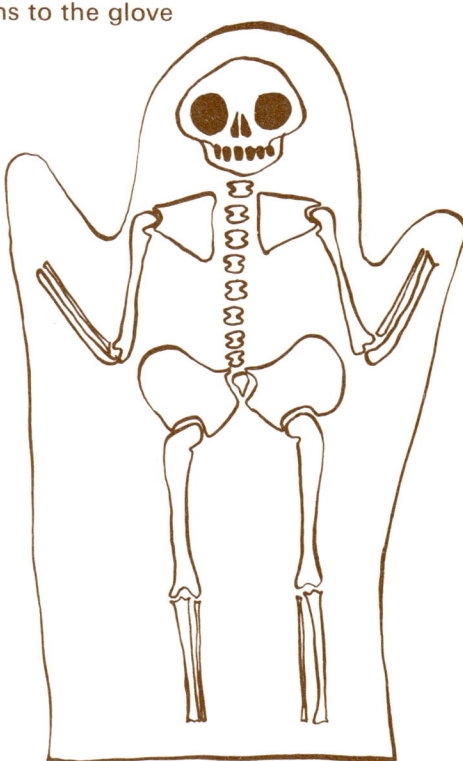

Figure 24

8   Stick the collar bones to the glove
9   Stick the ribs to the glove

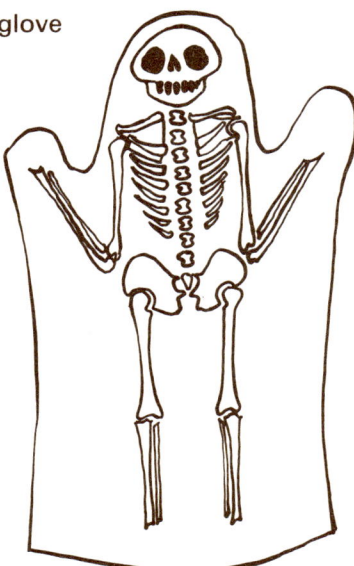

10 Stick the hands to the glove
11 Stick the feet to the glove

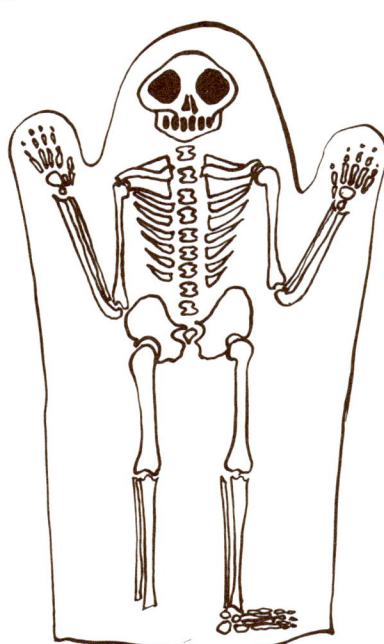

Figure 25

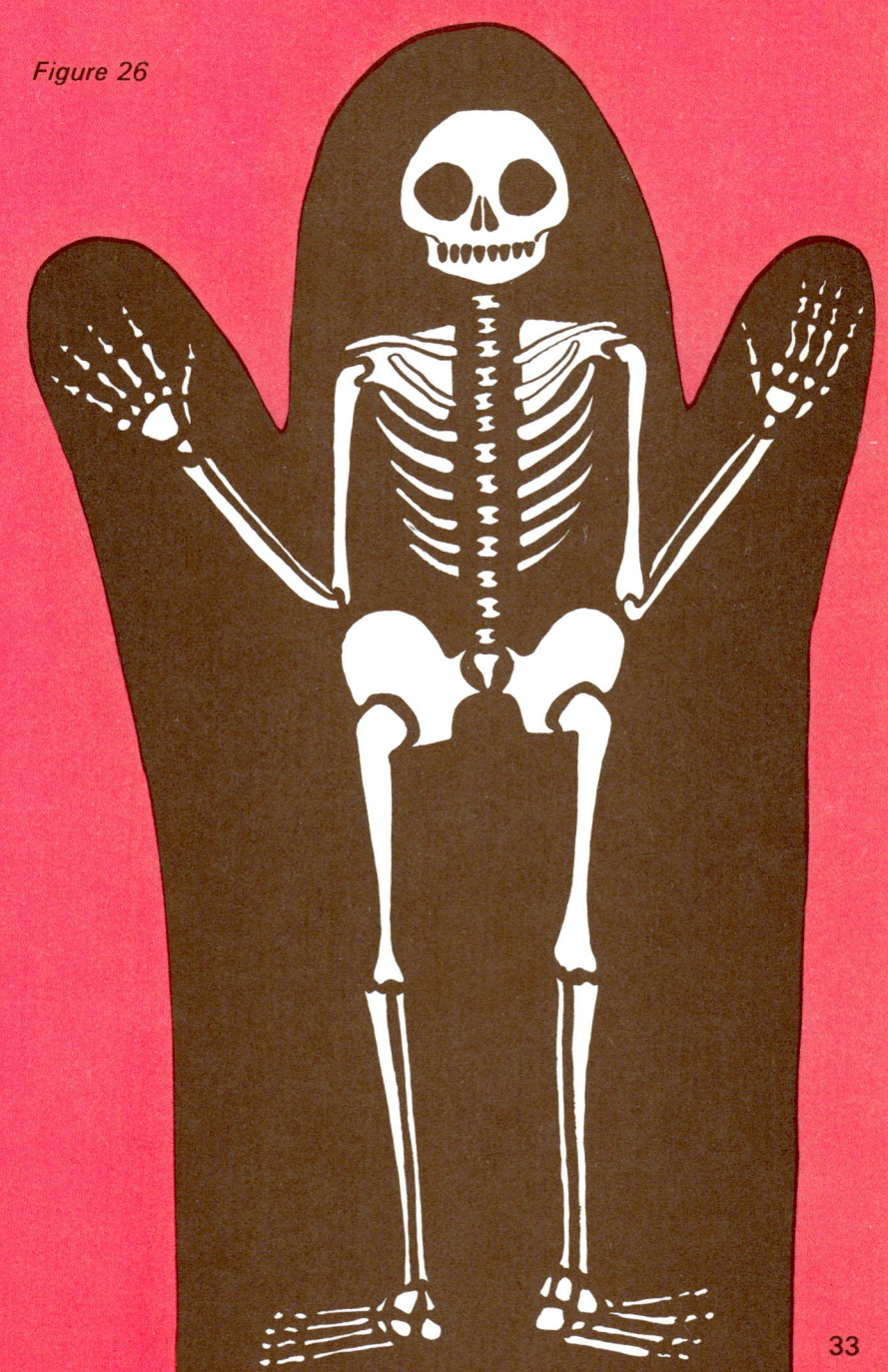
Figure 26

Finger Puppet   Bear

Basic shape
Cut two of these

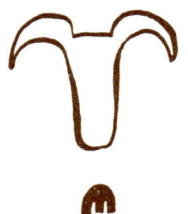

Muzzle

Nose

Cheeks

Chin

Eyes
Pupil

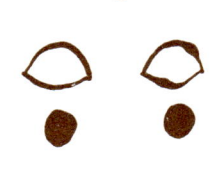

Ears

Inner ears

Figure 27

Cut out the basic shapes, see *figure* 27
Sew them together round the curved edge. Leave the straight edge open
Cut out all the features in *figure* 27
1   Stick the pupils to the eyes

2   Stick the outer ears to the inner ears

3   Stick the muzzle to the basic shape
4   Stick the cheeks to the basic shape

5   Stick the chin to the basic shape
6   Stick the eyes to the basic shape

7   Stick the nose to the muzzle
8   Stick the ears to the basic shape

Figure 28

Finger Puppet   Clown

Basic shape

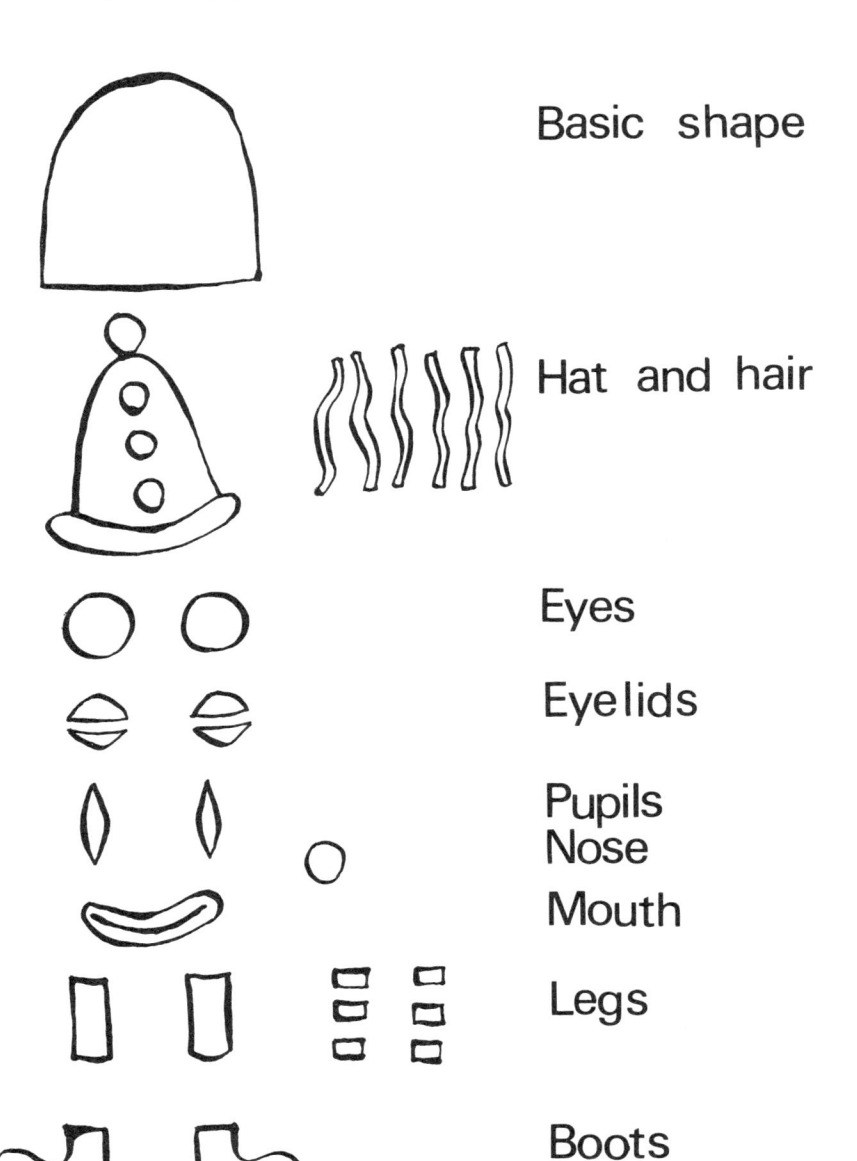

Hat and hair

Eyes

Eyelids

Pupils
Nose

Mouth

Legs

Boots

Figure 29

36

Cut out and sew the basic shape
Cut out all the pieces in *figure 29*
1 Stick the hair to the basic shape
2 Stick the stripes to the legs
3 Stick the legs to the boots
4 Stick the tops of the legs to the inside front of the basic shape

5   Stick the pom-pons to the hat
6   Stick the hat to the basic shape
7   Stick the eyelids to the eyes
8   Stick the pupils over the eyelids
9   Stick the eyes to the basic shape
10 Stick the nose to the basic shape
11 Stick the mouth to the basic shape

12 Make two small bows with thin wool and stick them to the top of the boots

Figure 30

Finger Puppet   Indian Girl

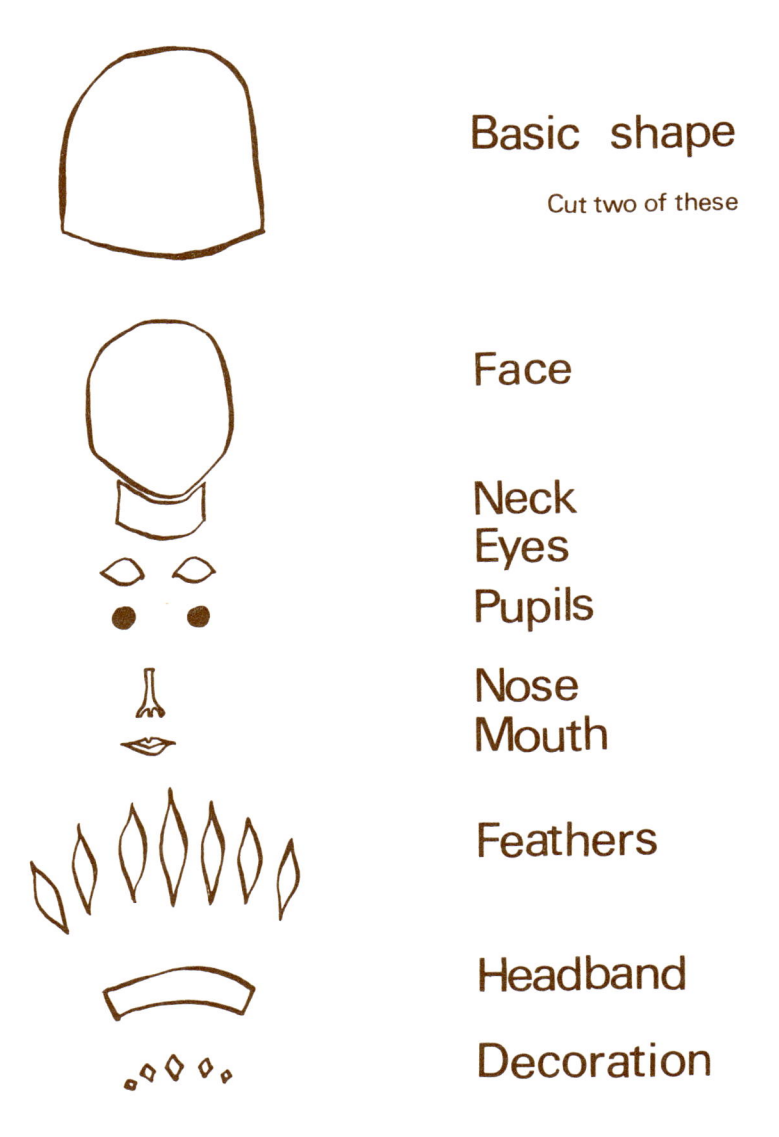

Basic shape

Cut two of these

Face

Neck
Eyes
Pupils

Nose
Mouth

Feathers

Headband

Decoration

Figure 31

Cut and sew the basic shape
Cut out all the pieces in *figure 31*
1 Stick the pupils to the eyes
2 Stick the eyes to the face
3 Stick the nose to the face
4 Stick the mouth to the face
5 Stick the face to the basic shape
6 Draw in the eyebrows,
with a black ballpoint pen
7 Stick the neck to the basic shape

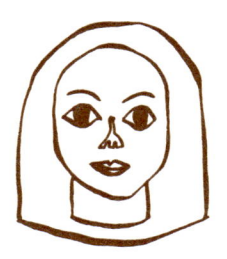

8 Using about six strands of fine wool, sew the hair to the top of the forehead and plait it as in the girl glove puppet

9 Stick the feathers to the headband
10 Stick the decoration to the headband
11 Stick the headband to the basic shape

Figure 32

Figure 33

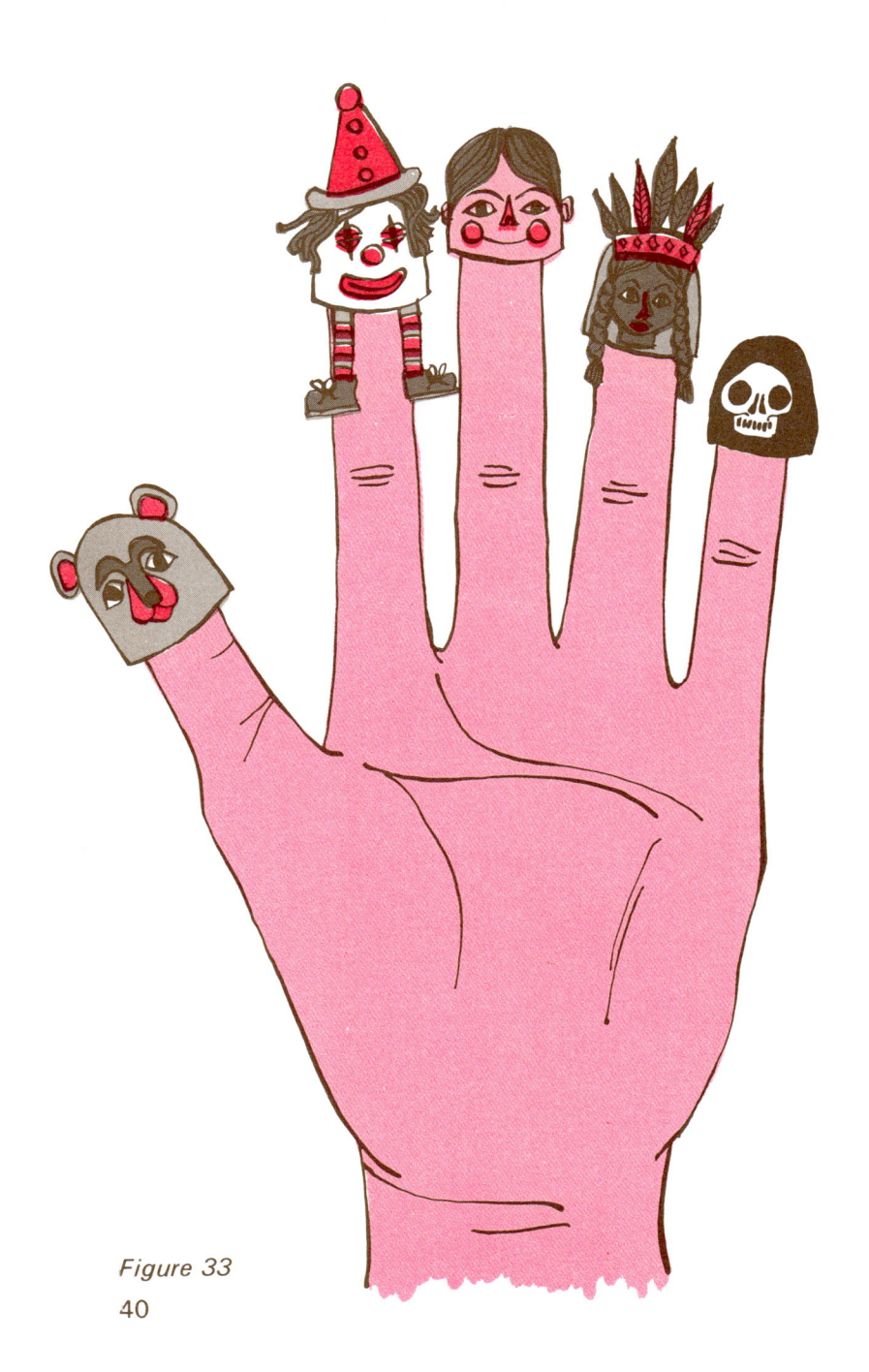

Finger Puppet Ideas

Figure 34

Stuffed Animal   Mouse

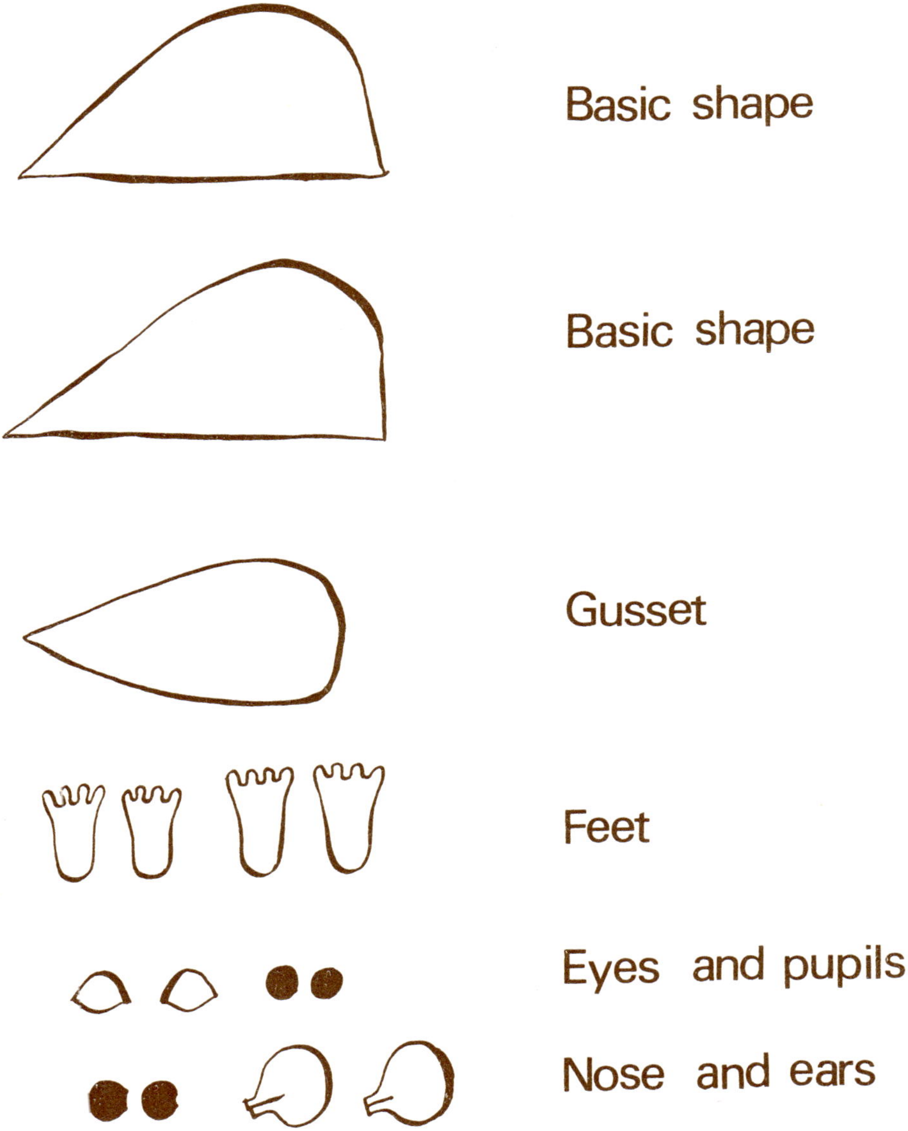

Basic shape

Basic shape

Gusset

Feet

Eyes and pupils

Nose and ears

Figure 35

Cut two of the basic shapes and the gusset, see *figure 35*
Sew the basic shape together along the curved edge. Leave edge
a open. See *figure 36*

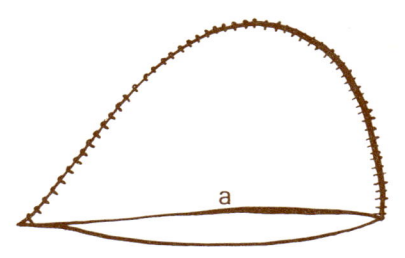

Fit the gusset into the open edges
Sew the gusset in, leaving a gap at *x*

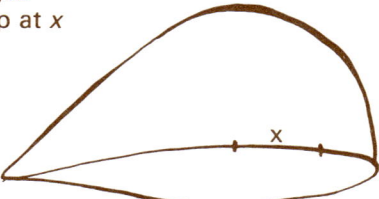

Stuff firmly with kapok, pushing the kapok well into the basic shape
Close the gap

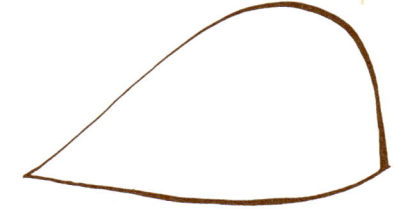

Figure 36

1   Sew a length of rug wool onto the rounded end of the basic shape
2   Stick the pupils onto the eyes

3   Stick the eyes onto the basic shape
4   Stick the nose onto the basic shape
5   Cut the ears where shown and overlap them
7   Stick the feet onto the underside of the basic shape. Point the toes outwards
8   Sew three loops of thread through each side of the nose. Snip the loops

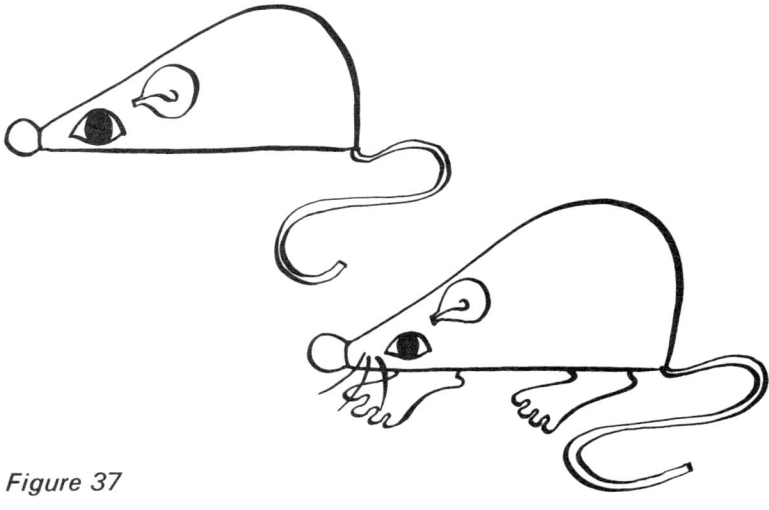

Figure 37

Figure 38

Stuffed Animal Hedgehog

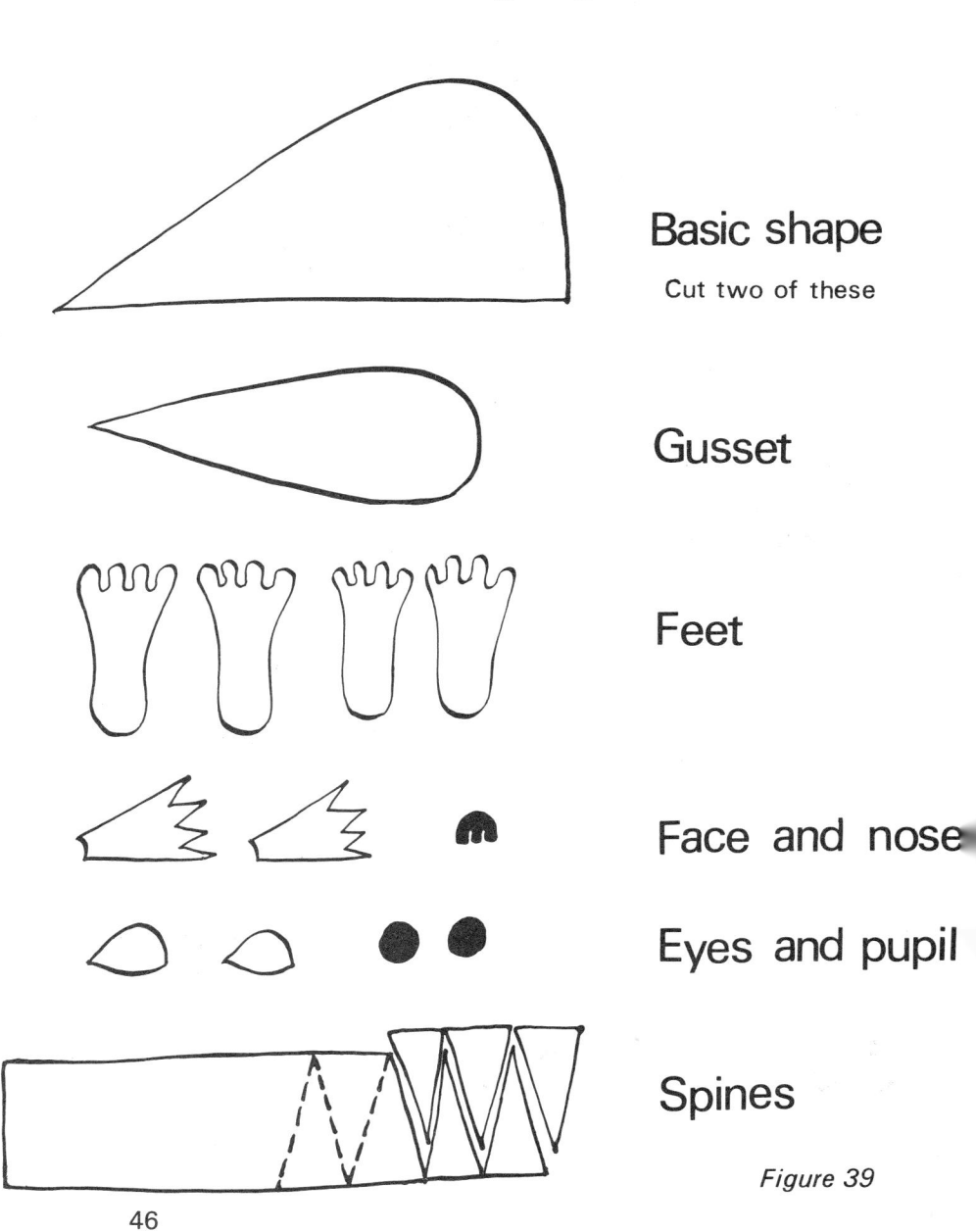

Basic shape
Cut two of these

Gusset

Feet

Face and nose

Eyes and pupil

Spines

Figure 39

Cut two basic shapes and the gusset
Sew and stuff them as in the instructions for the mouse

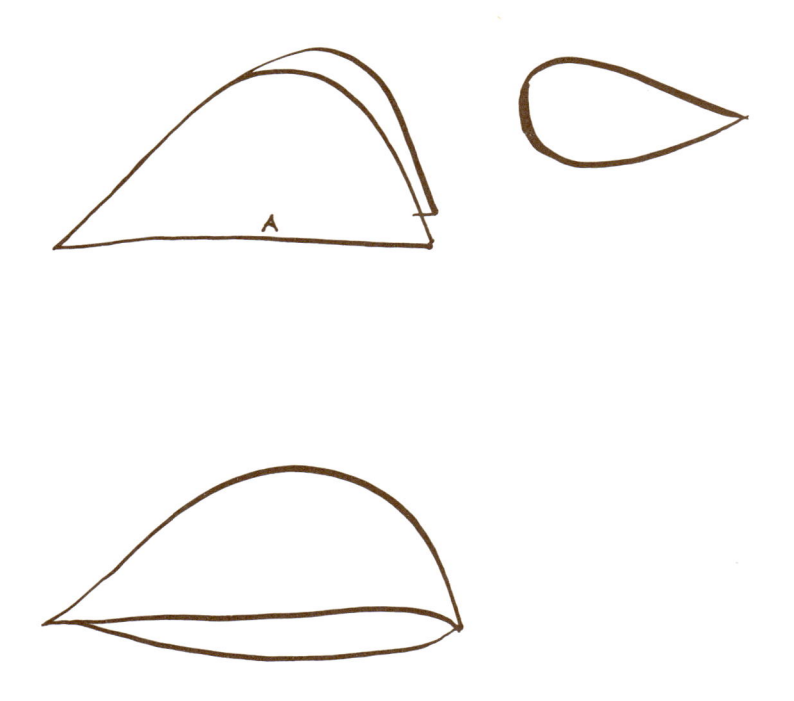

1   Cutting the spines as you need them, stick them on in overlapping rows, starting at the back of the basic shape, see *figure 40*

Figure 40

2   When the body is covered with spines, finish sticking them on, leaving a straight edge around the face
3   Stick the nose onto the basic shape

4   Stick the two face shapes onto the basic shape
5   Stick the feet onto the underside of the basic shape, pointing the toes outwards

6   Stick the pupils onto the eyes
7   Stick the eyes onto the face

Figure 41

Figure 42

49

Stuffed Animal   Oozle

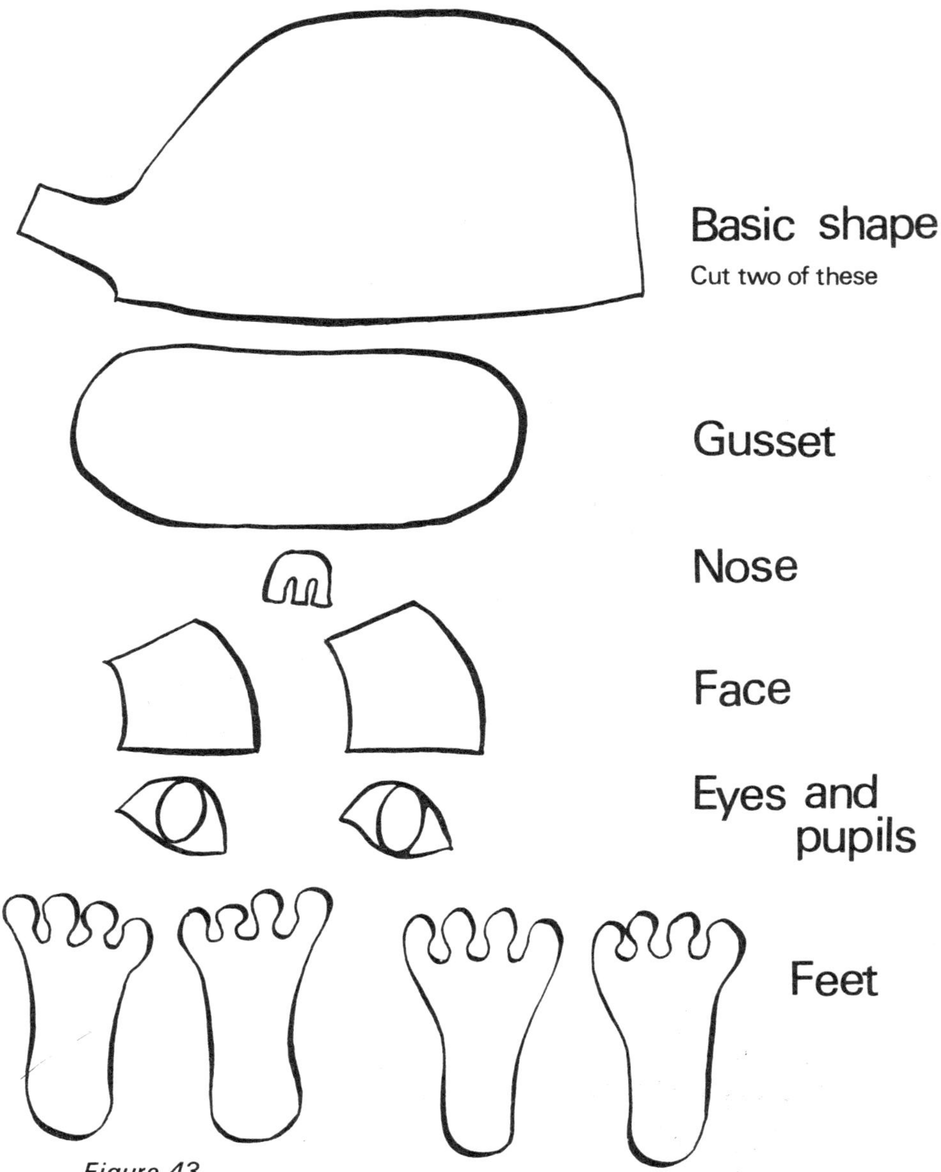

Basic shape
Cut two of these

Gusset

Nose

Face

Eyes and pupils

Feet

Figure 43

Cut two basic shapes
Cut out the gusset
Sew the basic shapes together and fit the gusset in as in the mouse. Stuff the basic shape firmly, pushing the stuffing well into the nose See *figure 44*

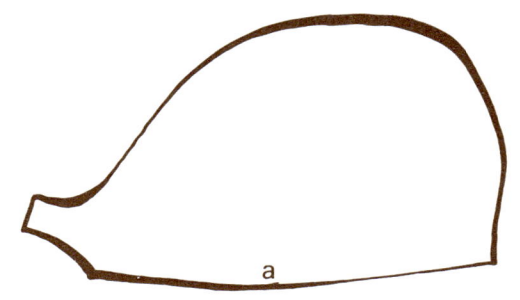

1   Stick the pupils to the eyes
2   Stick the eyes to the faces

3   Stick the faces to the basic shape
4   Stick the nose to the basic shape
5   Stick the feet to the underside of the basic shape pointing the toes outwards

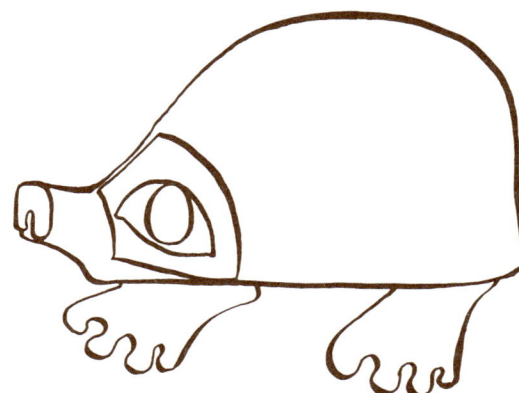

Figure 44

6 Stick a row of strands of rug wool round the basic shape

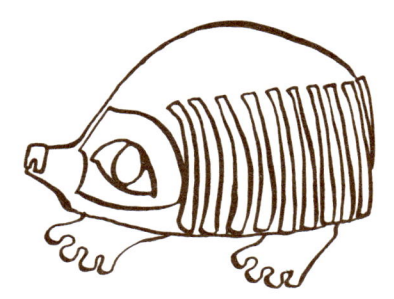

7 Continue sticking rows of wool round the basic shape until they meet at the top
8 Cut some strands of rug wool in half. Stick these onto the basic shape so that they make a fringe over the face
9 Stick a longer strand of rug wool along the back of the basic shape so that it covers the join where the other strands meet
10 Sew three loops onto each side of the nose. Snip the loops

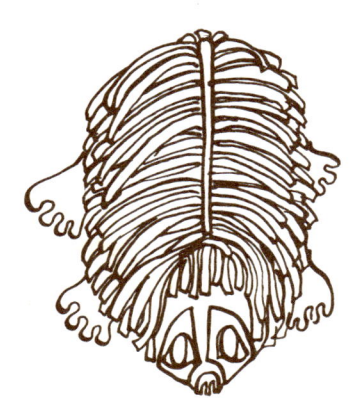

Figure 45

Figure 46

Stuffed Animal **Snake** *Figure 47*

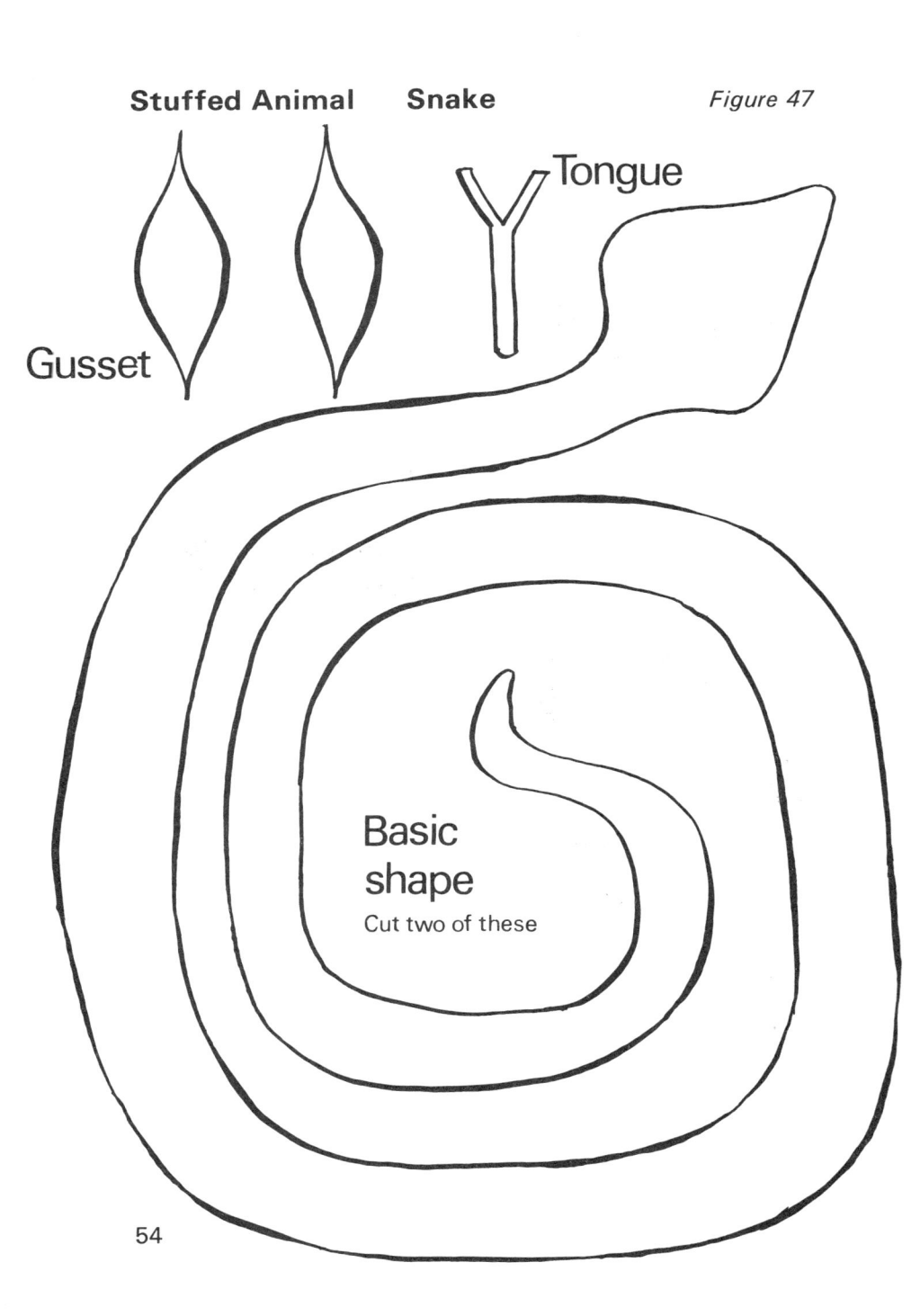

Tongue

Gusset

Basic shape
Cut two of these

Cut out two basic shapes and two gussets
Sew the gusset into the sides of the head
Sew the gussets into the sides of the head

Sew the basic shapes together along the entire length, see *Figure 48*, leaving gaps at *a*
Fill the snake with uncooked rice, starting at the tail and closing the gaps as you go,
OR
Stuff the snake with kapok, pushing it firmly into the body, again starting at the tail and closing the gaps as you go

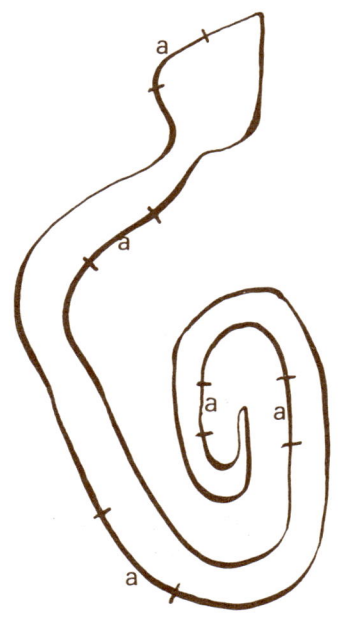

Figure 48

Figure 50

1 Sew the tongue to the head

2 Cut out two leaf shaped pieces of felt
3 Stick them to the upper side of the head
4 Sew a button into the centre of each leaf shape
5 Decorate the sides of the head, (the gussets) with contrasting felt
6 Decorate the body with contrasting felt

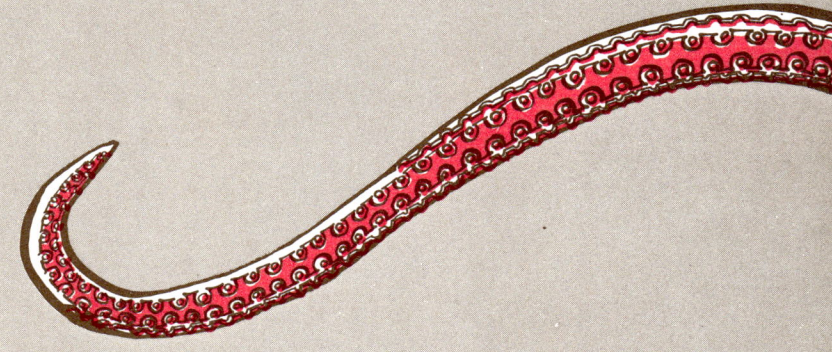

Figure 49

57

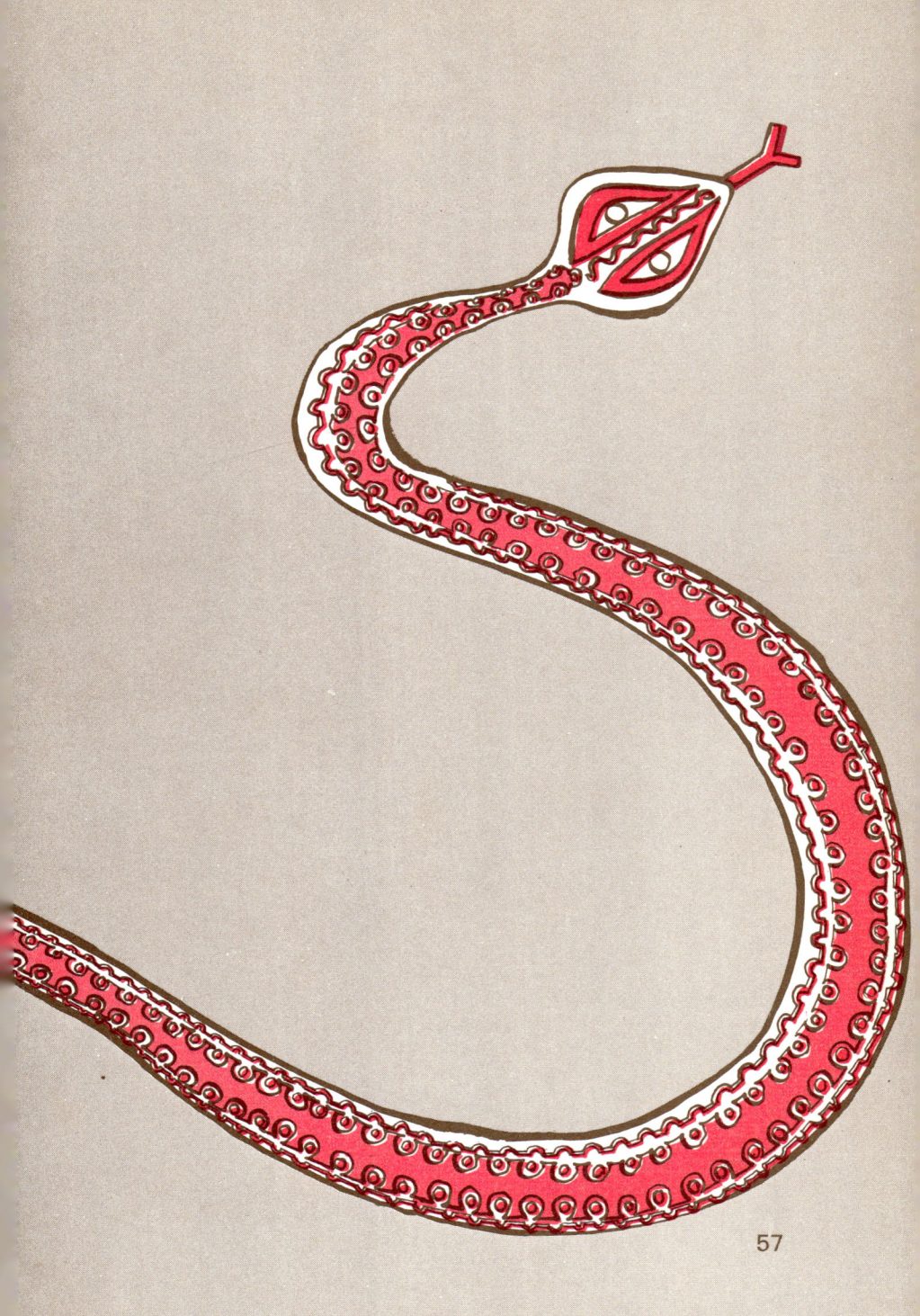

Stuffed Animal   Tortoise

Basic shape
Cut two of these

Head

Feet

Tail

Shell pattern

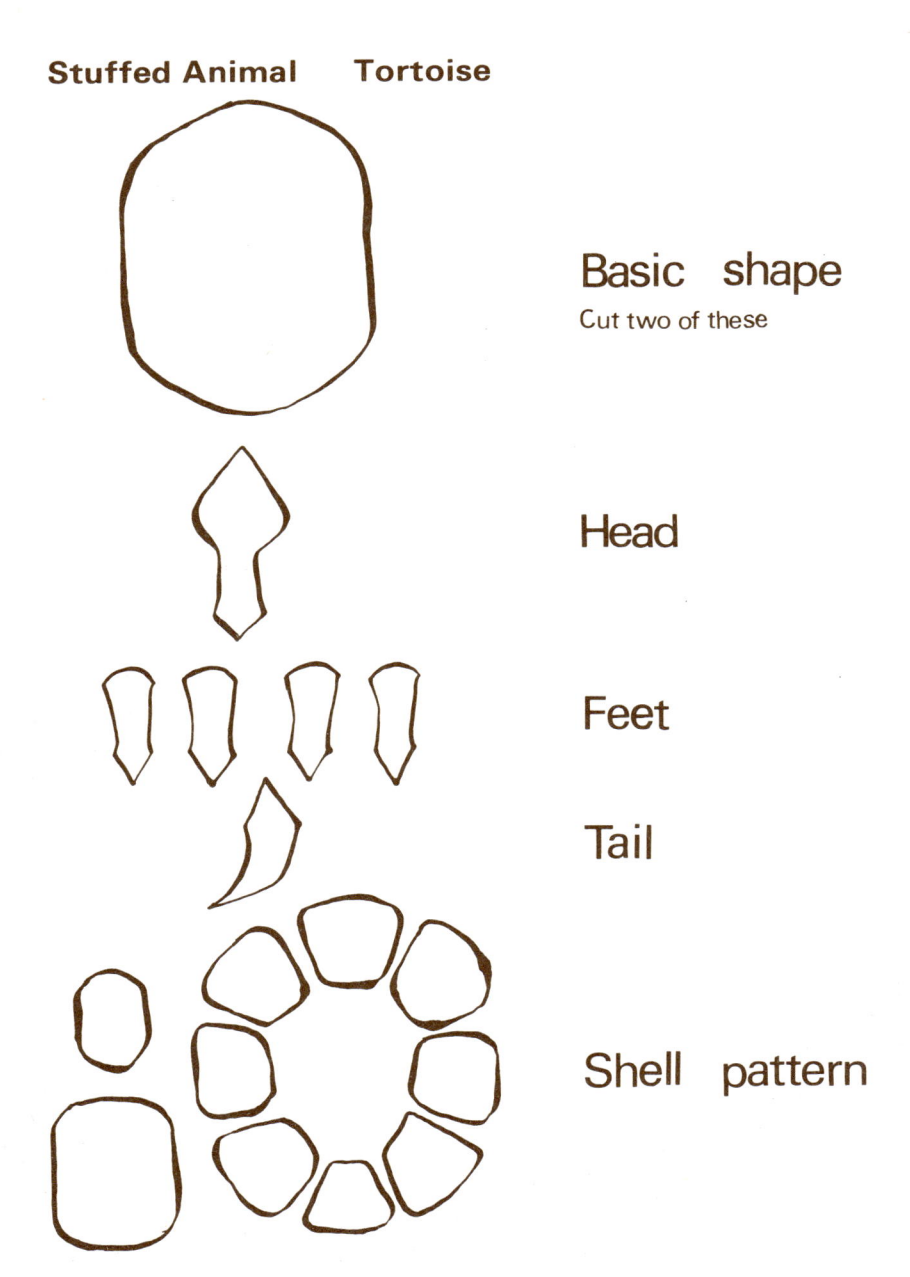

Figure 51

Cut out the basic shapes and all the other pieces in *figure 51*
Sew the two basic shapes together, leaving a gap at *a,* see *figure 52*
Stuff the basic shape firmly with kapok
Close the gap

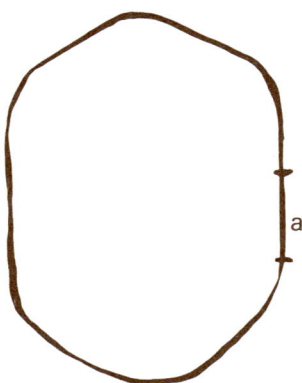

Cut out two small leaf shapes in felt
1   Stick the leaf shapes to the head
2   Sew a small button into the middle of each leaf shape
3   Stick the head to the basic shape
4   Stick the legs to the basic shape
5   Stick the tail to the basic shape

Figure 52

59

6 Stick the shell pattern onto the basic shape, starting with the outer scales and sticking the central scale on last
7 Cut out tiny semi-circles of felt and stick them onto the feet
8 Decorate the shell with contrasting felt or beads

Figure 53

To make the head and legs solid, cut out each piece twice, sew them together and stuff them. Sew onto the basic shape

Figure 54

Stuffed Animal   Owl

Basic shape
Cut two of these

Beak

Gusset

Outer eyes

Inner eyes

Feet

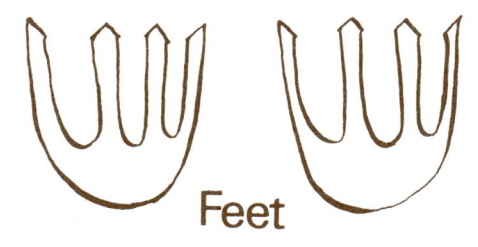

Pupils

Figure 55

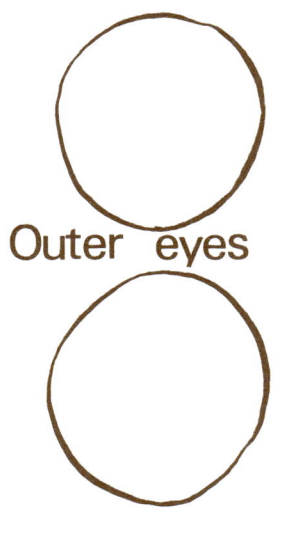

Cut two basic shapes, and the gusset

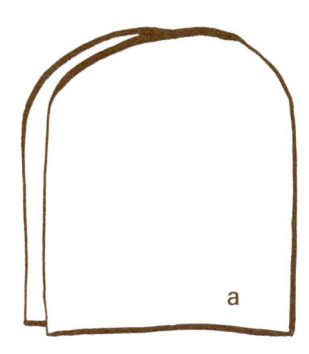

a

Sew and stuff the basic shape as in the mouse, see *figure 56*
Cut out all the other pieces in *figure 55*, except the feathers

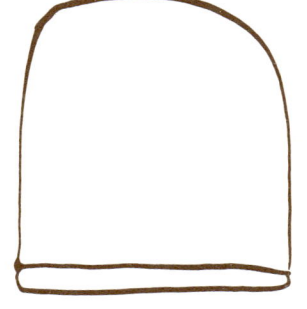

Figure 56

63

Cutting the feathers as you need them, and starting at the bottom of the basic shape
1   Stick the feathers on in overlapping rows
2   When the feathers are about half way up the basic shape, start to turn them, leaving spaces for the eyes
3   Continue sticking the feathers onto the basic shape until it is covered. Leave the eye spaces empty
4   Stick the beak onto the basic shape, between the eye spaces
5   Make little cuts in from the edges of the outer eyes
6   Stick the outer eyes into the eye spaces

7   Stick the pupils to the inner eye
8   Stick the inner eyes to the outer eyes
9   Stick the feet to the underside of the basic shape

Figure 57

Figure 58

Stuffed Animal   Broccoli Bird

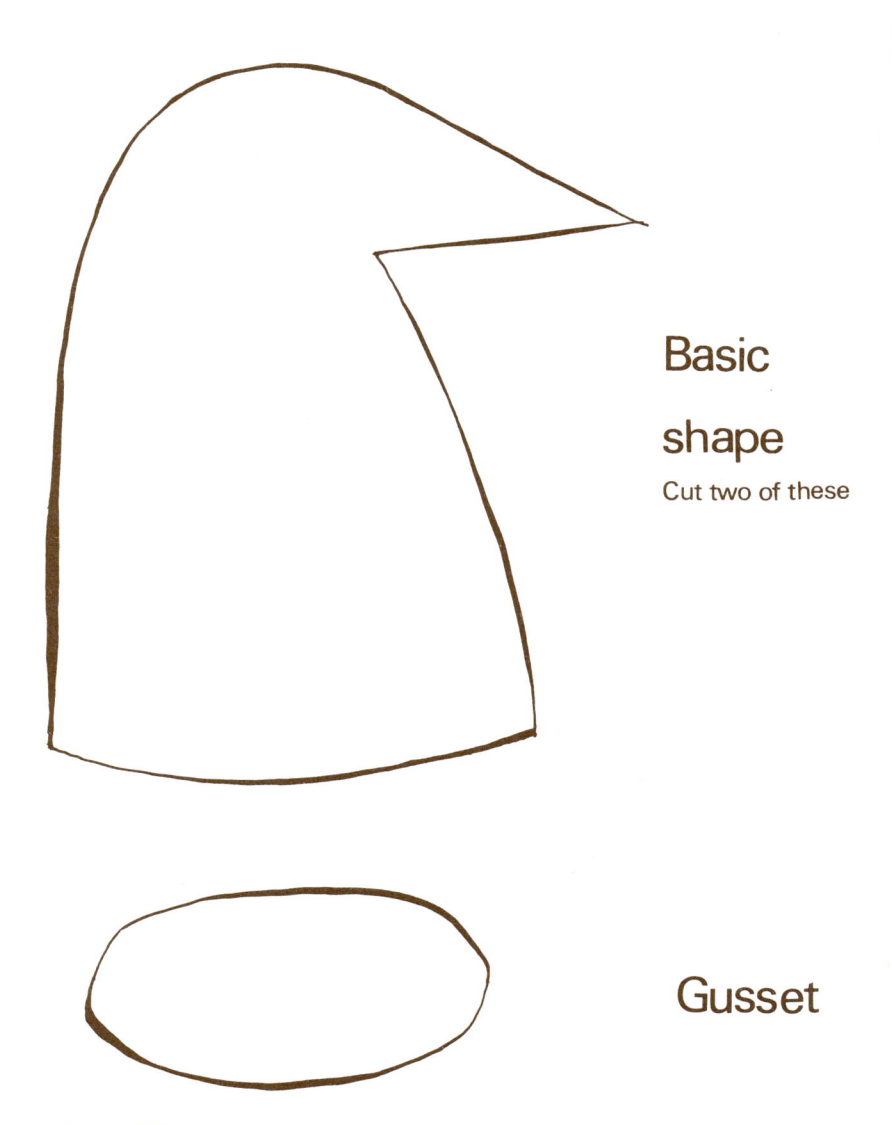

Basic shape
Cut two of these

Gusset

Figure 59

Leg Leg

Outer eyes

Inner eyes

Pupils

Feet

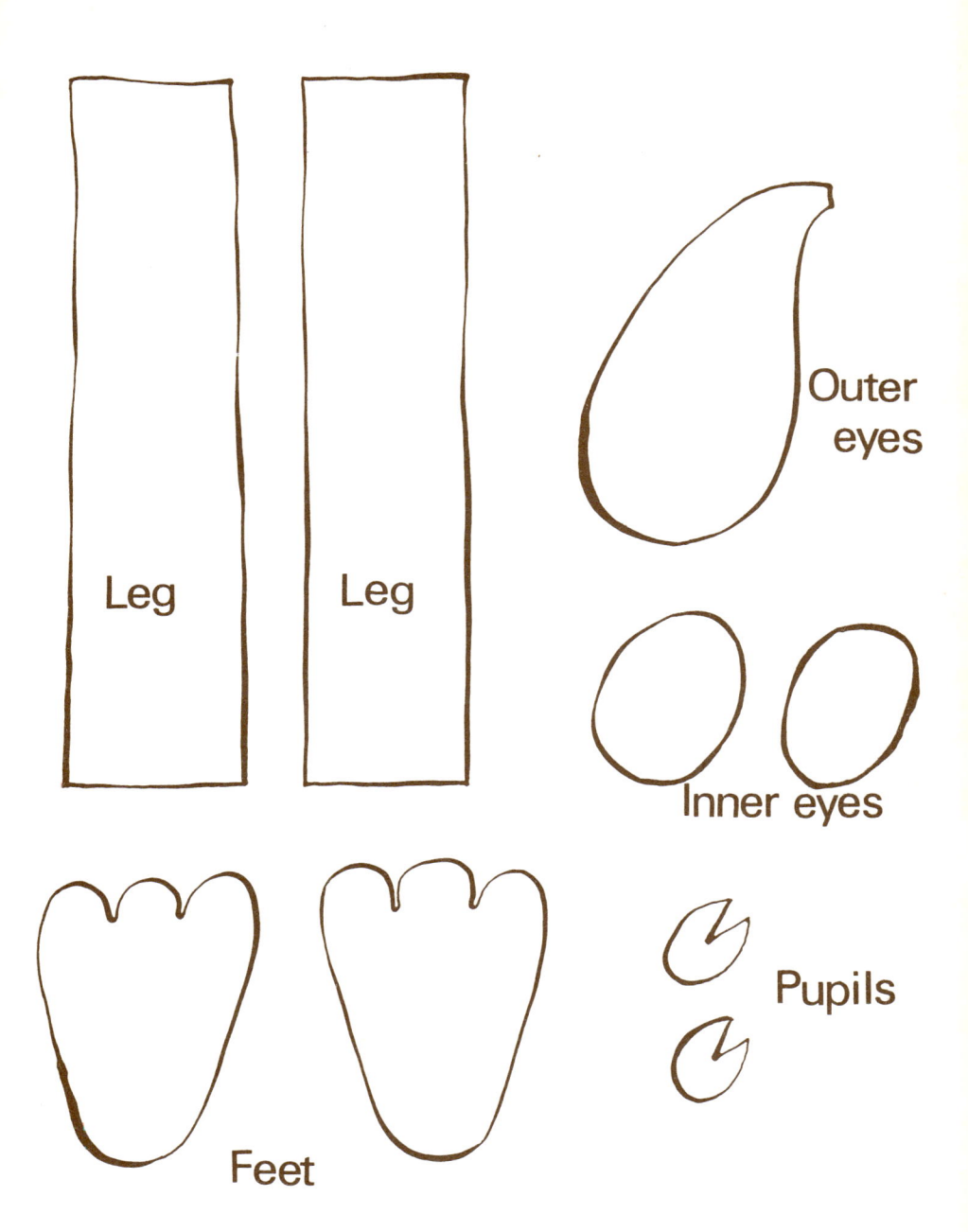

Figure 60

Cut two basic shapes, two legs, two outer eyes, two inner eyes, two pupils, four feet and one gusset, see *figures 59* and *60*
Sew the basic shapes together, leaving a gap at x, and fitting the gusset into side a, see *figure 61*

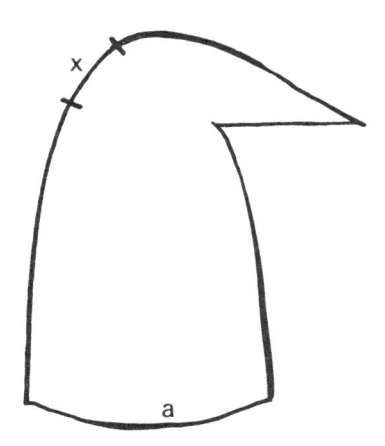

Stuff the basic shape firmly with kapok, pushing the stuffing well into the beak. Close the gap
Roll each leg into a cylinder and catch-stitch down the side

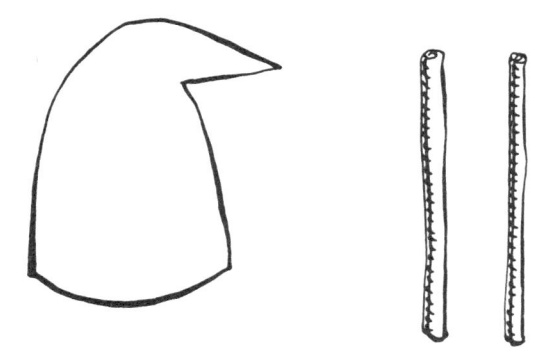

Figure 61

Sew the two halves of each foot together, leaving a gap at *a*, see *figure 62*
Stuff each foot firmly with kapok and close the gap
Sew each leg to each foot

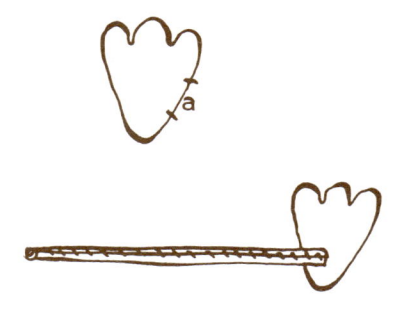

Sew the other end of each leg to the underside of the basic shape

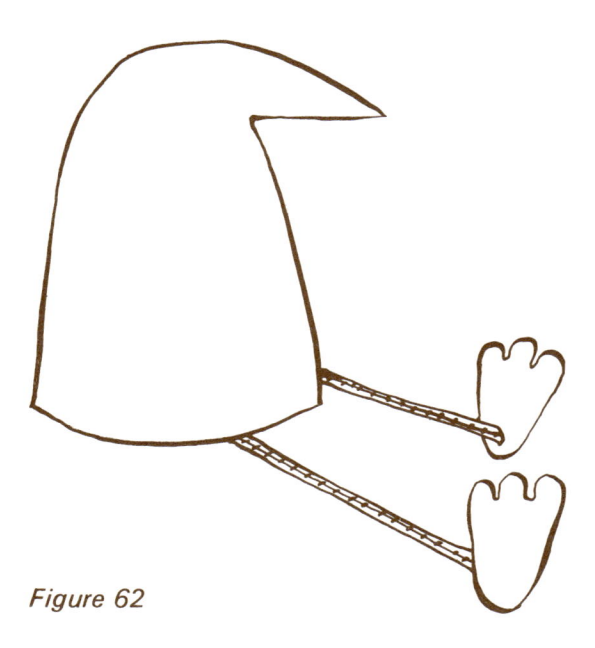

Figure 62

69

Cut the feathers as you need them
1   Starting at the base of the basic shape, stick the feathers on in overlapping rows

2   When you reach the eye space, turn the feathers as in the owl

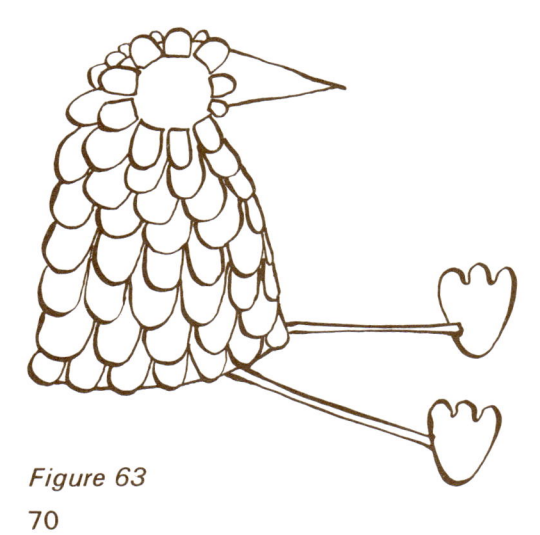

Figure 63

3 Stick the pupils to the inner eyes
4 Stick the inner eyes to the outer eyes

Figure 64

5 Stick the outer eyes into the eye spaces
6 Cut several curving strips of contrasting felt for the tail
7 Stick these to the underside of the basic shape at the back

Figure 65

Figure 66

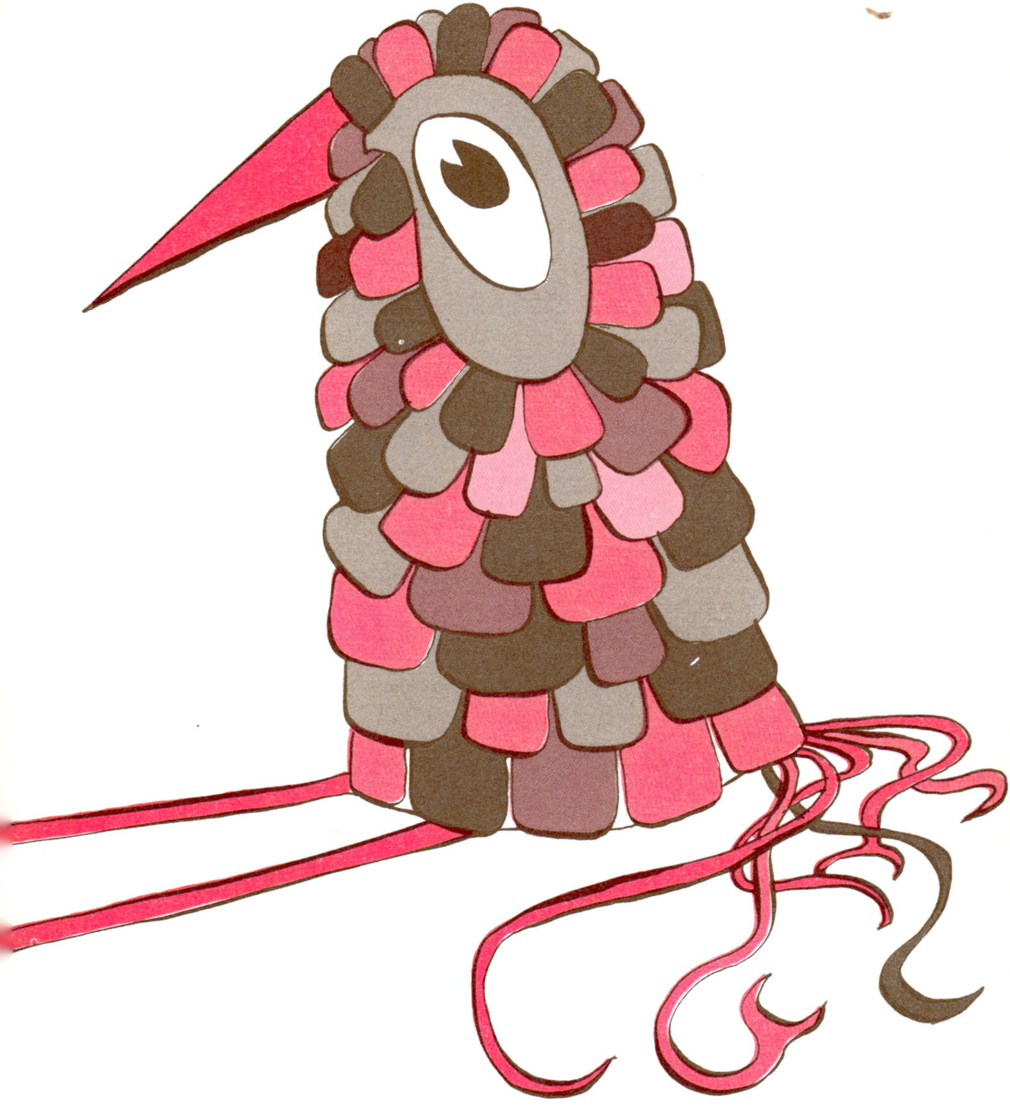

Stuffed Animal   Lizard

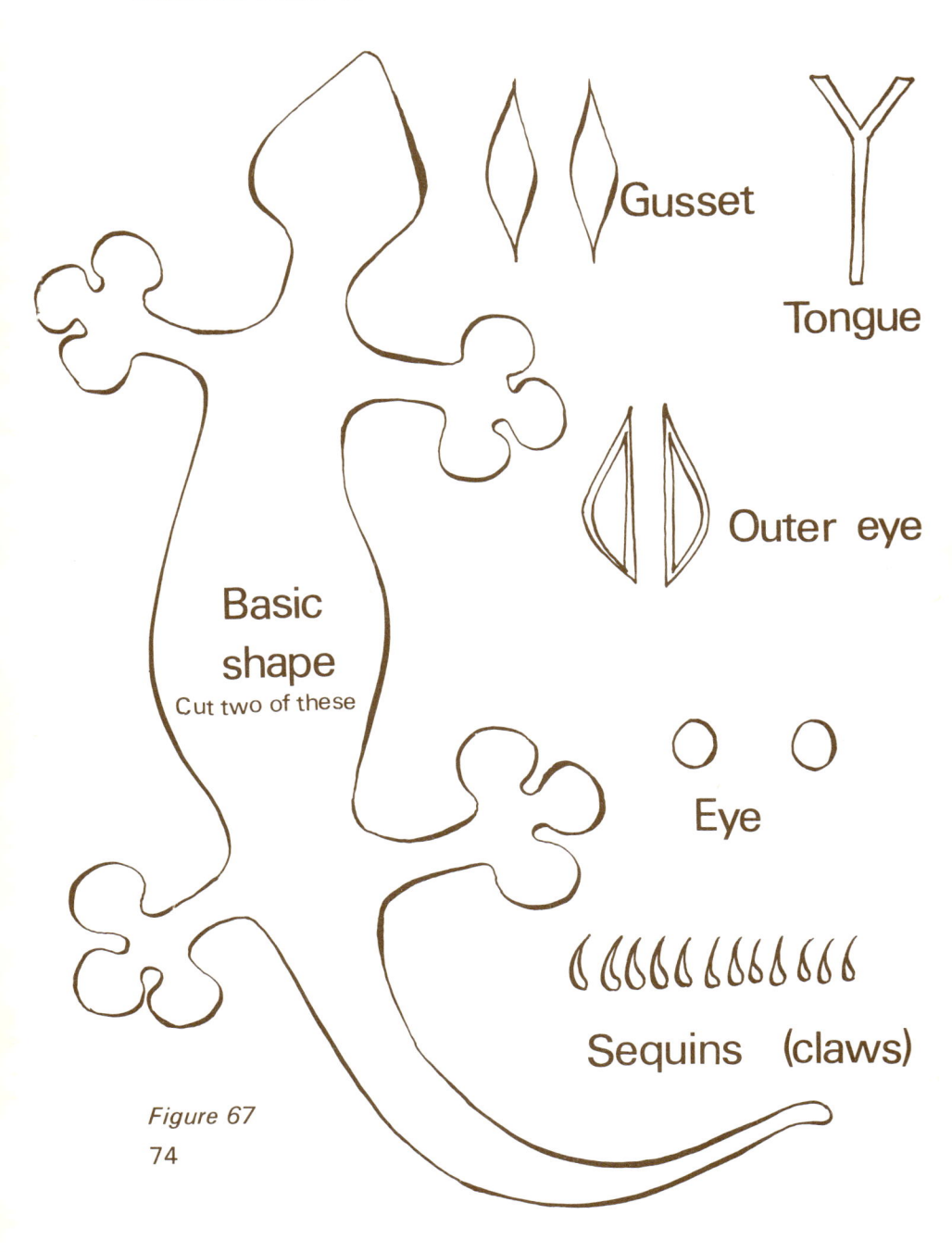

Gusset

Tongue

Outer eye

Basic shape
Cut two of these

Eye

Sequins (claws)

Figure 67

Cut two basic shapes and two gussets
Fit the gussets into each side of the head, sew the basic shapes together, leaving gaps at a, see *figure 68*
Fill the lizard with uncooked rice, starting at the tail and closing the gaps as you go
OR
Stuff the lizard with kapok, starting at the tail and again, closing the gaps as you go

1   Stick the two outer eyes onto the head
2   Sew a button into each outer eye
3   Sew three claw sequins onto each foot

Figure 68

4   Cut patterns and decorations in contrasting felt. You can make these up as you go along

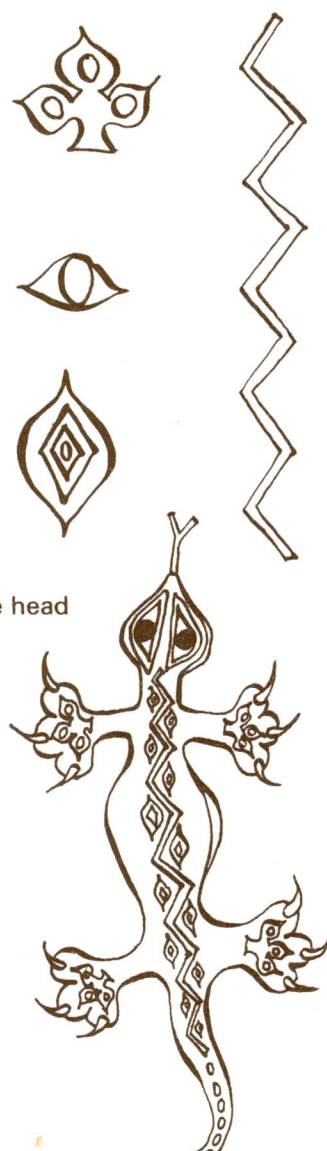

5   Stick these onto the lizard
6   Sew the tongue to the tip of the head

Figure 69

Figure 70

Stuffed Animal   Dragon

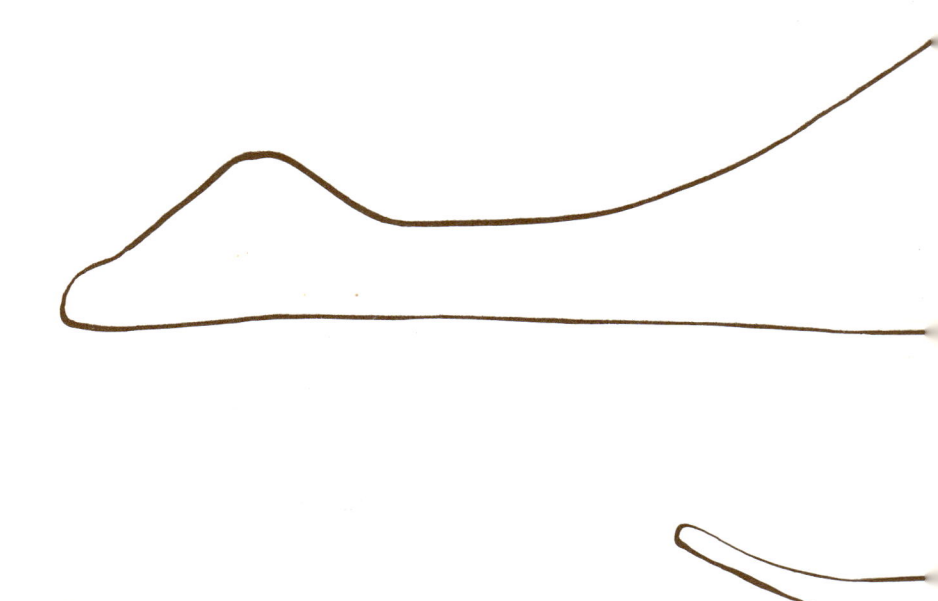

Gusset

Figure 71

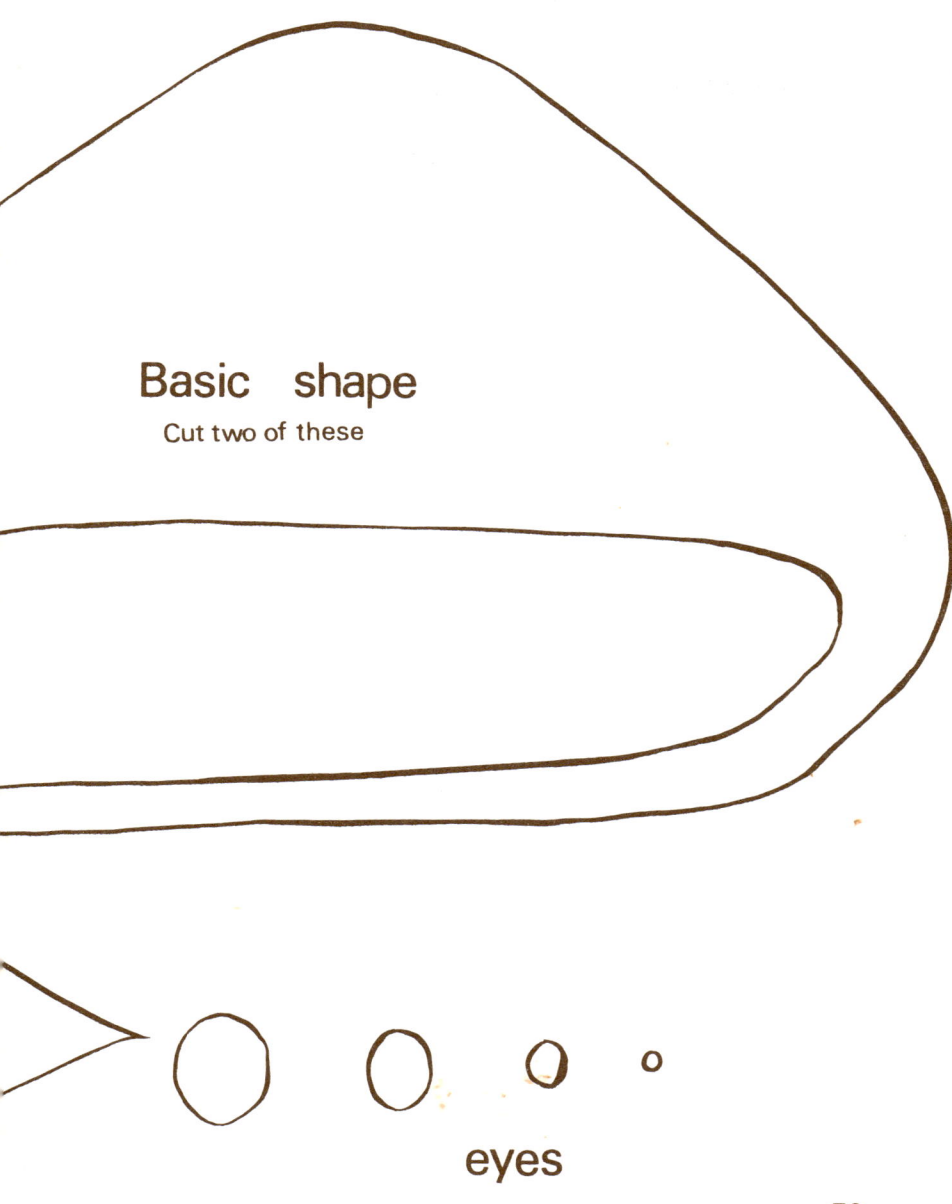

Basic shape
Cut two of these

eyes

79

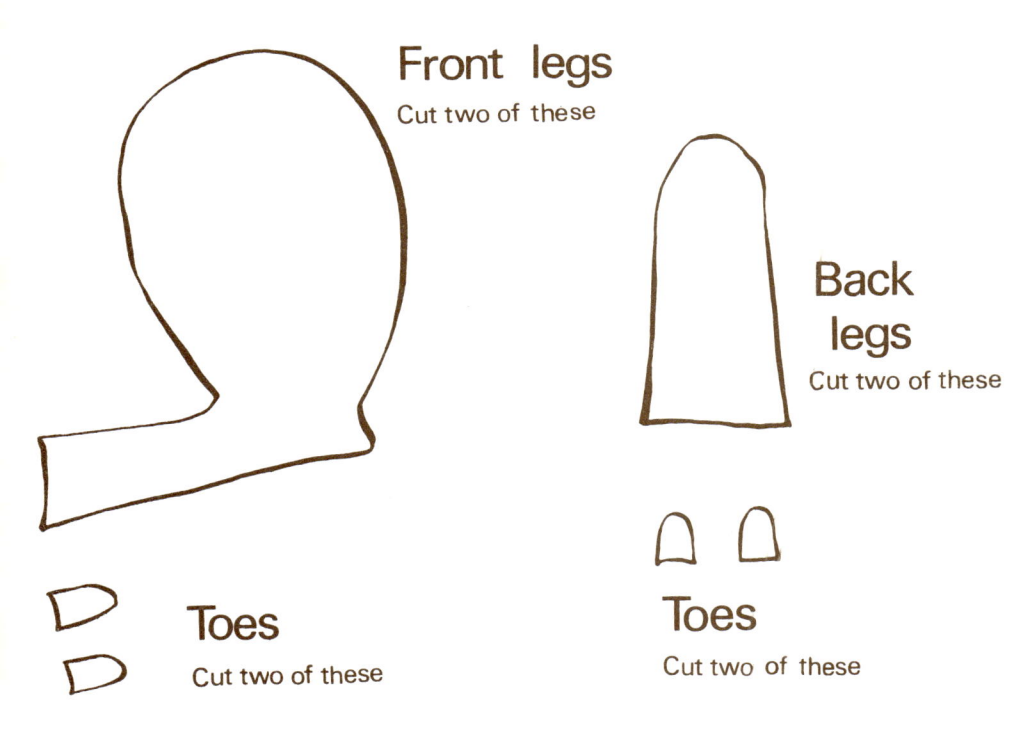

Tail spike
Cut two of these

Decoration
Cut two of these

Front legs
Cut two of these

Back legs
Cut two of these

Toes
Cut two of these

Toes
Cut two of these

Figure 72

Cut out all the pieces in *figures 71* and *72*. It is very effective if you cut the eyes, legs, tail spike and tail decoration in a slightly paler shade of the colour chosen for the basic shape
Sew the basic shapes together, starting at the tip of the nose and sewing along the top of the back, the top of the tail, round under the tail, and leaving a space at *a*. See *figure 73*
Measure the gusset against the basic shape, and continue sewing, leaving a gap large enough to fit the gusset in

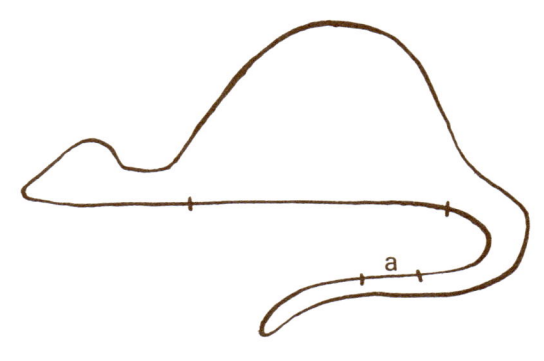

Fit the gusset into the gap and leave a space for putting the stuffing in
Stuff the head of the dragon first, then the body, closing the gap in the gusset. Then stuff the tail, closing the gap in the tail when you are satisfied that the basic shape is firm enough
Pull the tail round to the side of the body and make two tiny stitches at the base, to hold it firmly

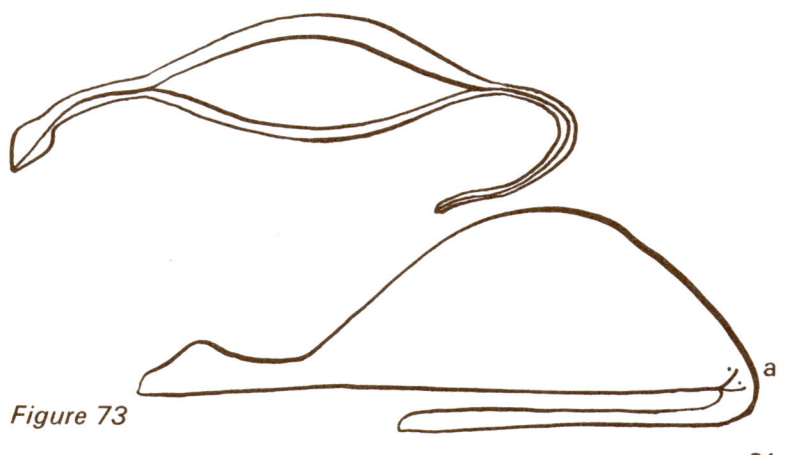

Figure 73

1   Stick the eye pieces together

2   Stick the eye onto the basic shape
3   Stick the tail spike onto the tail, one spike each side, with the tail sandwiched in between
4   Stick the decoration onto the tail spike

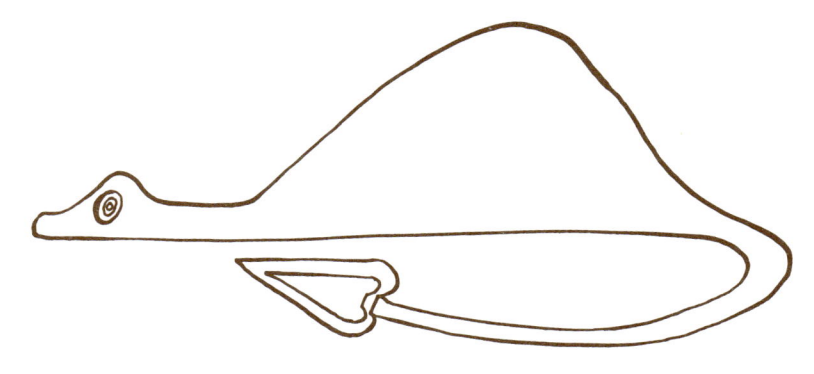

5   Cut a long strip of felt, (long enough to go from just behind the head to the tip of the tail)
6   Cut spikes on one side of the strip
7   Sew the strip down the back of the basic shape

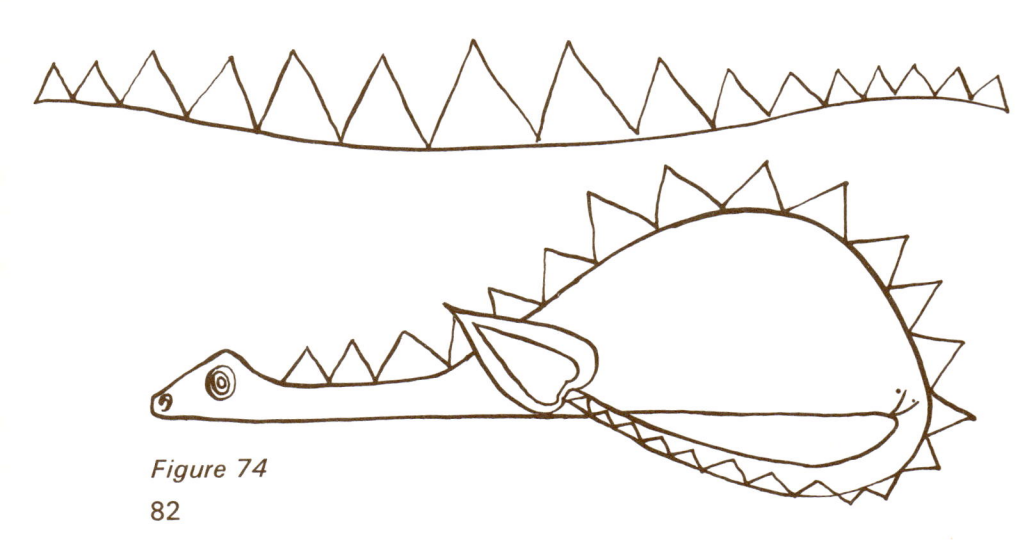

Figure 74

8 Stick the toes to each leg
9 Stick the legs onto the basic shape

10 Sew a ruff of claw sequins behind the head of the dragon

Figure 75

83

Figure 76

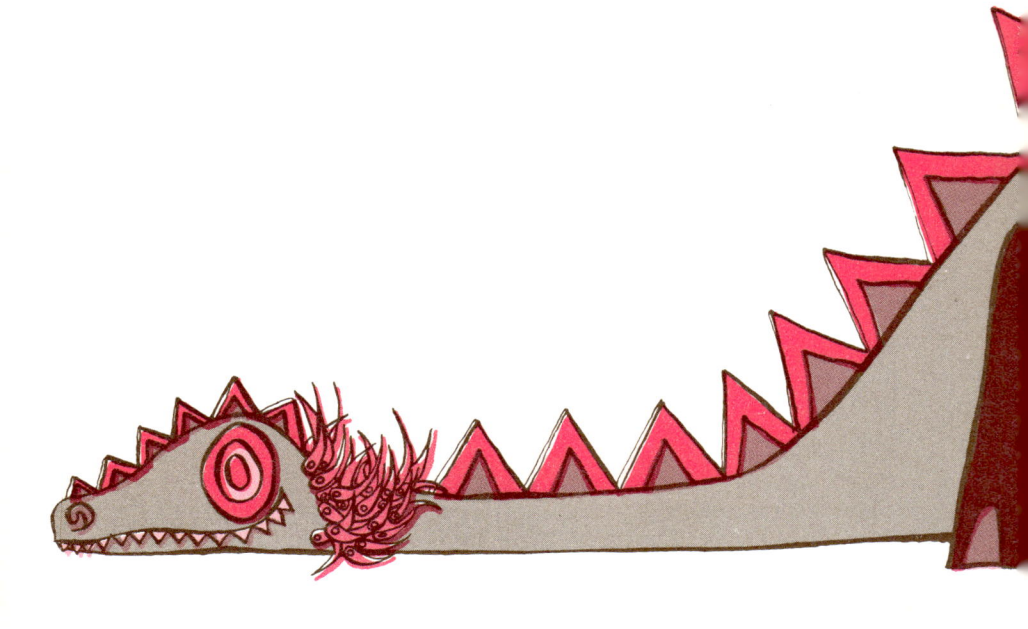

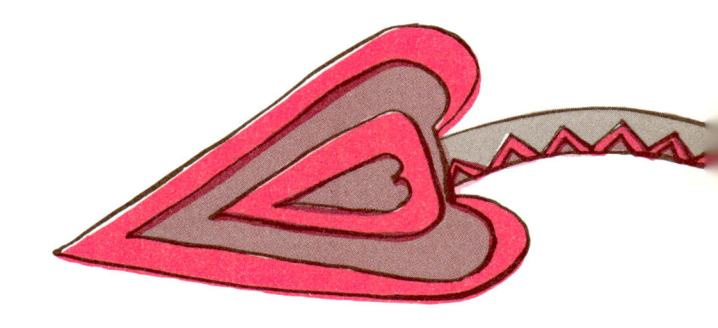

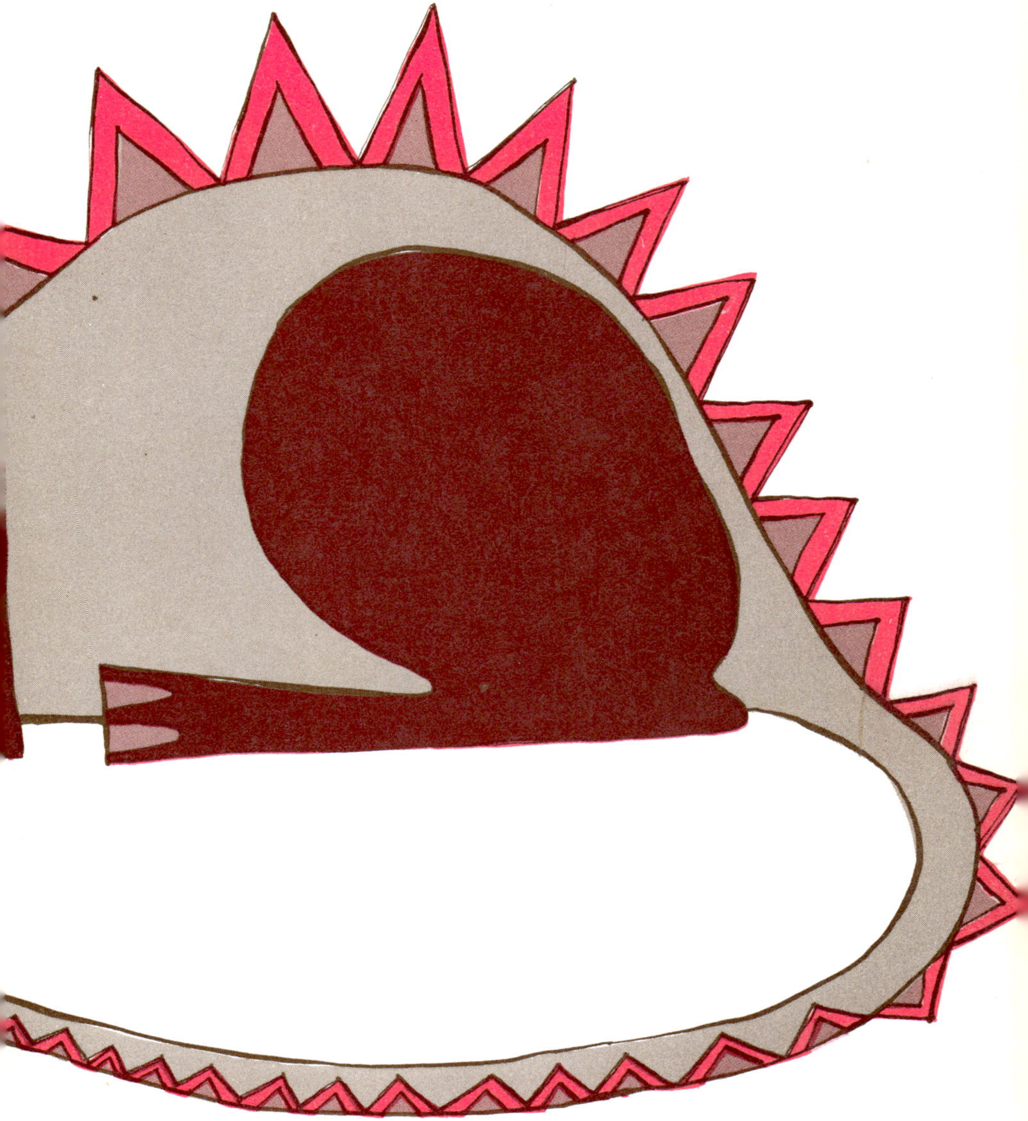

More Ideas

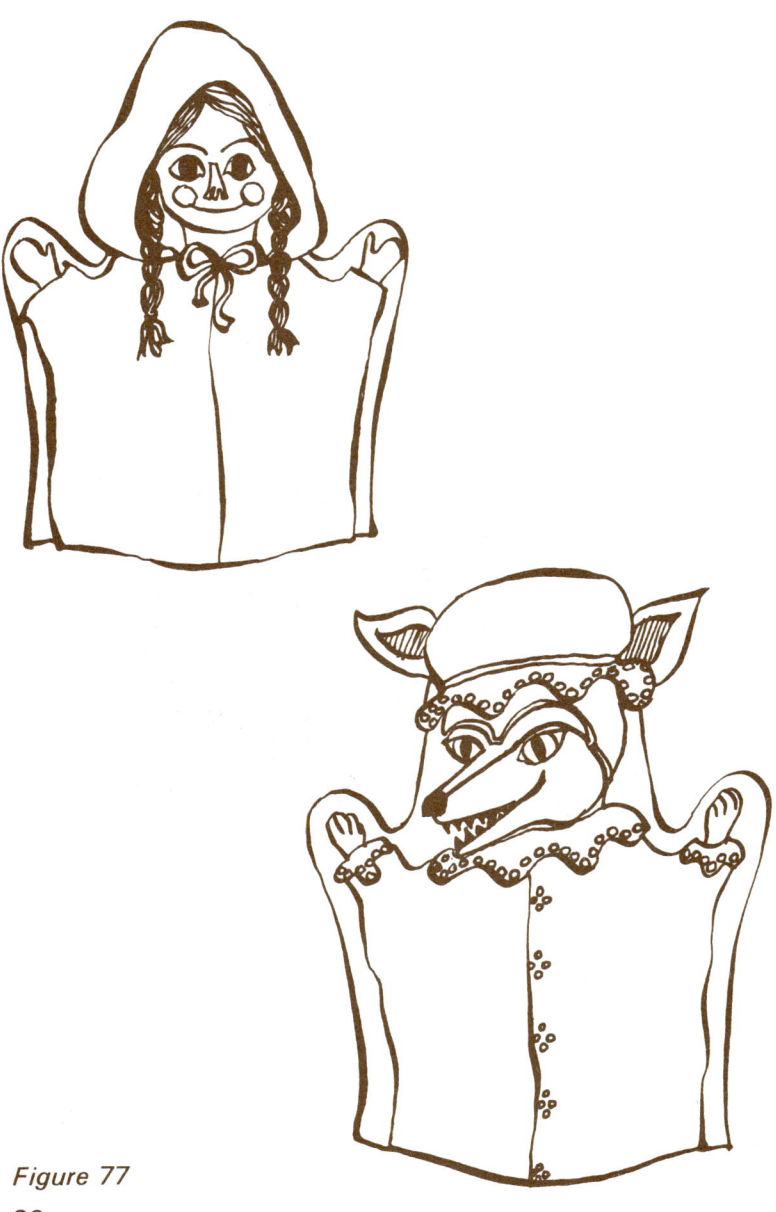

Figure 77

Figure 78

Suppliers

Felt

Fred Aldous Limited
The Handicraft Centre
37 Lever Street   Manchester M60 1UX

Arts and Crafts
10 Byram Street   Huddersfield HD1 1DA

Home Pastimes Handicrafts
69 Mansfield Road   Nottingham

Dryad Handicrafts Limited
Northgates   Leicester

Leighton, Baldwin and Cox
41 High Street   Leighton Buzzard   Bedfordshire

The Felt and Hessian Shop
34 Greville Street   London EC1

Squares of felt can usually be bought at any large department store

Paton and Baldwins
76 Grovenor Street   London W 1

Rug wool

Rug wool can usually be bought from most large wool shops

Glue

Copydex is available from most stationers and hardware shops

Kapok

Woolworth Limited

Sequins

Pickaby claw sequins are available from most department stores